# BE
# YOURSELF!

# BE YOURSELF!

## THE CALL
## OF A
## CHRISTIAN

**MAURITIUS WILDE, OSB**

Paulist Press
New York / Mahwah, NJ

Cover design by Dawn Massa, Lightly Salted Graphics
Book design by Sharyn Banks

Originally published in Germany as *Zeigt Euch!*, Copyright © 2015 by Vier-Türme GmbH-Verlag; English translation by Peter Dahm Robertson, Copyright © 2019 by Paulist Press

Library of Congress Cataloging-in-Publication Data

Names: Wilde, Mauritius, author.
Title: Be yourself! : the call of a Christian / Mauritius Wilde, OSB.
Other titles: Zeigt Euch! English
Description: New York : Paulist Press, 2019.
Identifiers: LCCN 2018041658 (print) | LCCN 2018056306 (ebook) | ISBN 9781587686801 (ebook) | ISBN 9780809153312 (pbk. : alk. paper)
Subjects: LCSH: Witness bearing (Christianity)—Catholic Church. | Christian life—Catholic authors.
Classification: LCC BX2347.4 (ebook) | LCC BX2347.4 .W5513 2019 (print) | DDC 248/.5—dc23
LC record available at https://lccn.loc.gov/2018041658

ISBN 978-0-8091-5331-2 (paperback)
ISBN 978-1-58768-680-1 (e-book)

Published by Paulist Press
997 Macarthur Boulevard
Mahwah, New Jersey 07430
www.paulistpress.com

Printed and bound in the
United States of America

# CONTENTS

# PREFACE
## A KEY EXPERIENCE

When I was taking my first cautious steps as the head of our German monastery's publishing house, I had a key experience at the Frankfurt Book Fair. As a monk, I did not have a great deal of clothing appropriate for such an event. So, I bought a sports coat for the occasion—when in Rome, do as the Romans do. Then, finally walking the halls of the Book Fair, I ran into a monk in a brown habit.

I was about to greet him enthusiastically, when I realized he was not a monk at all. He was an "eyecatcher." The friendly man was quick to confirm my impression: his job was to hand out pamphlets and to attempt to draw visitors' attention, only to maneuver them to the stand behind him, where they would look at the products on offer.

I was shocked—and then annoyed. Why was I, who had been a monk for more than two decades and was representing a monastery publishing house, sneaking around "disguised" as a civilian so as not to stand out, while a "fake" monk was actively drawing all the attention toward him? Why was I reluctant to proclaim confidently who I was and what I was representing? Why did I not show what and in whom I believed? Those questions gave me a great deal to think about, and over time, I tried to change.

# ACKNOWLEDGMENTS

For suggestions and inspiring conversations, I offer heartfelt thanks to: Br. Thomas-Morus Bertram, OSB; Abbot Jeremy Driscoll, OSB; Dr. Matthias E. Gahr; Fr. Konrad Göpfert, OSB; Dean Kuno Kuhn; Fr. Thomas Leitner, OSB; Pastor Willy Manzanza; Regina Nothelle; Sr. Dr. Julia Prinz, VDMF; Abbot Jeremias Schröder, OSB; Br. Ansgar Stüfe, OSB; the participants of the courses "Wenn ich nach meinem Glauben gefragt werde" and "New Evangelization—Task and Joy"; my editor, Marlene Fritsch; Br. Linus Eibricht, OSB, and the team at the Vier-Türme-Verlag; as well as my fellow brothers in Münsterschwarzach, Germany, and in Schuyler, Nebraska.

# INTRODUCTION
## AN ABUNDANT HEART

I can still vividly remember a young couple whom I had the joy of accompanying on their way to marriage. I encouraged the two to pray together, as well. "Pray together? Isn't that too intimate?" they asked. At first, I had to smile at that, given that I had figured that intimacy should be possible in a marriage. But then I understood that it was a real problem: most of society's taboos have fallen, but religion and death are among the few that remain. One just doesn't talk about religion. Religiousness and spirituality are "private matters"—so private that one does not talk about them with one's own partner.

Yes, praying is intimate; praying together even more so. One is opening oneself up before the other and making oneself vulnerable. That may be what prevents us from showing our faith externally. We are afraid, and we may even be somewhat ashamed. Having a faith—maybe even "needing" one—is considered a weakness.

Even though religiousness is something within us, this is not something external or foisted upon us that we would truly need to be ashamed of. Faith is about what I believe, who I am in my innermost heart. It is a question of what is in my heart or weighing on it. The Gospel of Matthew tells us, "Out of the abundance of the heart the mouth speaks" (Matt 12:34). It isn't good to constantly hold back what is in our hearts. If your heart is full, let it overflow!

Now, you may object that it is not so simple. A young grandmother told me that she wanted to pass her faith on to her granddaughter but felt constrained by the fact that the mother had no use for religion. This is understandable. So how can we find the right, fitting, respectful language with which to express something of our faith?

Many people use small signs that point to their faith or their beliefs: a necklace with a cross, a bumper sticker with a fish on it. Many others use the dim light of a church to surreptitiously light a candle for a loved one or to pray for something that is troubling them. These are good rituals that can strengthen our faith, and seclusion is a space where our desire for the divine can be in good hands.

But when we encounter the world outside, things become less laid-back. We are faced with these questions: Should I invite my friend to the service? How can I tell my partner or my family and friends that I want a church wedding or want my child baptized? How do I react to the looks I get when I tell people I work for a religious day care center? Should I hang my cross at home so that friends who are visiting can see it as well? Should we as a family pray before our meal, even when the guests at our table do not share our faith?

We certainly don't want to be put in the same corner with people who are too quick to utter the name "God" or who pray ostentatiously, nor do we want to be like members of sects that proselytize on the street—people whose ideas have become ideology, so that they declare all those who don't share their views either stupid or irresponsible. And we want even less to be confused with fundamentalists, to be too pious. Within all these constraints, is there any room left to express our faith?

Nevertheless, at least in my native Germany, more and more people—though very rarely Christians—are publicly expressing their faith. This gives public displays of faith nowadays an unpleasant aftertaste and exposes cultural differences with which we may not be entirely comfortable.

But is the Christian faith not also a "culture," a culture of love and respect? A culture that wants to have an outward effect, that wants to be *lived*? When we articulate our experiences or thoughts, share them with someone, show them outwardly, do they not also gain weight and greater significance for us as well? That may be the opportunity to express our faith: it confirms us in what we are convinced of anyway.

This book aims to encourage people to confidently proclaim their own faith. To that end, we will go to the one with whom it all began—Jesus Christ—and see what the Bible has to say about testifying, since proclaiming something always means bearing witness to it. We will also see the exciting journey that is ahead of us: a journey that can nourish and enrich our personal spirituality.

I am a monk. Normally, monks retreat and go within themselves. They tend to be introverts, and—as the opening story might have suggested—I am no exception to this rule. So, if you are still skeptical about going on this journey with me, be assured that I am on your side as an advocate. Paradoxically, monastic tradition means that monks especially have much to contribute to this question. By drawing on contemplation, prayer, and silence, they may even be best equipped to venture out into this world.

The congregation I belong to is known as the Missionary Benedictine Congregation of St. Ottilien. For years, we have been looking for the right balance between inwardness and the expression of our faith. The ways in which we offer faith speak to many people, since our monastery's guesthouses and the retreats offered there are full. So how can one connect contemplation with bearing witness? What can our mission as Christians look like in today's open, pluralist society?

In a speech before the cardinals, Pope Francis said something that touches us all as Christians: "When the Church does not come out of herself to evangelize, she becomes self-referent and then she gets sick. The evils that over the course of time happen in ecclesial institutions have their root in a self-reference and a sort of theological narcissism."[1] The gospel, however, calls us to go outside ourselves, to open ourselves and become fertile ground for others, to pass on the good we have been given.

Narcissism isn't just a Church problem, it's a societal one. As early as 1980, American historian and social critic Christopher Lasch diagnosed it as an illness of our times, and the wealth of current literature on the topic confirms his diagnosis.[2] So, in addition to our timidity, it is often also our self-obsession that keeps us from radiating something of the One who loves us far more than we could ever love ourselves. If we were to go outside ourselves, we as Christians could thus do a service to all people.

Jesus went outside of himself, out of his homeland, and beyond convention to spread the message that inspired him. He went out from the center—his Father, who loved him so deeply—to the people on the edges who needed this love desperately. He went to those who needed to change their ways so that they might not miss a life in fullness. He felt himself sent to the people: "Whoever welcomes me welcomes not me but the one who sent me" (Mark 9:37). "Sending" and "being sent" are the original meanings of the word *mission* (from the Latin *mittere*, "to send"). But, the Gospels tell us, it took thirty years for Jesus to begin his journey. Up to that point, he had lived an orderly life without attracting much attention, probably working with his adoptive father, Joseph, in the family business in Nazareth. In other words, we, too, should go only when we hear the call. But we should not miss that moment, either.

This book is not about concepts and strategies, but about faith and spirituality: How important for my faith and for me personally is it to go outside myself, and how can I do so? How do I find the right words? How do I bear witness without becoming defensive? Who can help me? What should I expect? How can I pass on my faith in a friendly, relaxed way, without becoming aggressive, manipulative, or preachy, without complaining or invading others' private life—but without having to be a saint, either?

Hopefully, this book will awaken us to the impulses of our heart that want to be let out so that we can express our faith in who we are. Whenever I give seminars on this subject, a lively conversation about what the individual participants have experienced in their faith will often start up quickly. That is what I wish for this book, as well: that it encourages us to return to conversation, that we have the courage to be ourselves.

1

# BON VOYAGE!

Professing one's faith is an exciting thing because it causes encounters. Orbiting oneself, however, is boring: the only person I ever meet is me. Revealing yourself and your faith is a journey, at least as it is described in the gospel. Jesus sees no problem with his disciples' displays of faith—quite the opposite: he encourages them. But he also gives them precise instructions that we will take as a blueprint here. One of the places where Jesus talks about bearing witness is the so-called Mission of the Seventy in the Gospel according to Luke. Let us take a journey along that road.

## THE MISSION OF THE SEVENTY

After this the Lord appointed seventy others and sent them on ahead of him in pairs to every town and place where he himself intended to go. He said to them, "The harvest is plentiful, but the laborers are few; therefore ask the Lord of the harvest to send out laborers into his harvest. Go on your way. See, I am sending you out like lambs into the midst of wolves. Carry no purse, no bag, no sandals; and greet no one on the road. Whatever house you enter, first say, 'Peace to this house!' And if anyone is there who shares in peace, your peace will rest on that person; but if not, it will return to you. Remain in the same house, eating and drinking whatever they

1

provide, for the laborer deserves to be paid. Do not move about from house to house. Whenever you enter a town and its people welcome you, eat what is set before you; cure the sick who are there, and say to them, 'The kingdom of God has come near to you.' But whenever you enter a town and they do not welcome you, go out into its streets and say, 'Even the dust of your town that clings to our feet, we wipe off in protest against you. Yet know this: the kingdom of God has come near.'"...

The seventy returned with joy, saying, "Lord, in your name even the demons submit to us!" He said to them, "I watched Satan fall from heaven like a flash of lightning. See, I have given you authority to tread on snakes and scorpions, and over all the power of the enemy; and nothing will hurt you. Nevertheless, do not rejoice at this, that the spirits submit to you, but rejoice that your names are written in heaven."

At that same hour Jesus rejoiced in the Holy Spirit and said, "I thank you, Father, Lord of heaven and earth, because you have hidden these things from the wise and the intelligent and have revealed them to infants; yes, Father, for such was your gracious will. All things have been handed over to me by my Father; and no one knows who the Son is except the Father, or who the Father is except the Son and anyone to whom the Son chooses to reveal him."

Then turning to the disciples, Jesus said to them privately, "Blessed are the eyes that see what you see! For I tell you that many prophets and kings desired to see what you see, but did not see it, and to hear what you hear, but did not hear it." (Luke 10:1-11; 17-24)

## Can I do this? Am I good enough?

*After this the Lord appointed seventy others.*

There are two initial questions: *Should* I proclaim my faith? And if yes: *Can* I proclaim my faith? In Luke, Jesus' speech gives a clear answer to both: Yes, you should! And: yes, you can (together with me)! It is Jesus, himself, who sends out the disciples. Would he send them if he did not trust them to do well? But this immediately poses another question: The Gospel does say that Jesus appointed seventy. Am I among these chosen ones? Sometimes, however, it can be off-putting to see people who are convinced that they are chosen and proclaim their faith so ostentatiously that it makes one cringe and not want to become like them.

I was once speaking with a family that had been doing a great deal of work in their congregation for years. We were talking about whether or not they were "following Jesus" in their life. They gave a clear answer: "No." I was astounded, since their actions had given me a different impression. But I could understand what they were trying to say: it was not that they did not love or revere Christ, but they saw following Jesus as a special field reserved for priests and members of religious orders— religious "professionals," as it were.

But in the gospel passage above, Jesus shows clearly that everything has been "hidden...from the wise and the intelligent and...revealed...to the infants." For Jesus, proclaiming your faith does not require several years of study. Quite the opposite. He has his doubts whether the intelligent understand what they are supposed to proclaim.

Our churches suffer from the wide gap between "amateurs" and "professionals." Often enough, the clergy draws a clear line and makes plain what lies in its—and *only* its— competence. This, of course, does not often include the laity into the fold. Within Catholic terminology, the word *laity* causes especially great confusion because it suggests that all nonclerics are incompetent and "amateurish." In fact, the term comes from the Greek word *laos* and simply means "the people": all people of God. Priests are laity, too! Of course, one can also find a comfortable space on the other side of this gap: "We've done our bit by going to church, now we expect something from the professionals!" After all, needing to position oneself might also become quite unpleasant at some point. The back benches of the church are more relaxed.

Jesus' solution is that faith belongs neither to one kind of believer nor the other. The revelation occurs between Father and Son. Only the Father knows who the Son is and only the Son knows who the Father is "and anyone to whom the Son chooses to reveal him." All "knowledge" that faith has to offer comes from Jesus and from him alone. He gives to whom he will. No one has any predominant rights to faith.

Jesus chose twelve apostles. *Apostle* means "person sent forth"—meaning that he especially entrusted them with carrying on the faith. But in our gospel passage, he selects seventy (or seventy-two) additional disciples. It seems evident that this number is symbolic. It is a number expressing a large quantity. That means that in Jesus' eyes, proclaiming one's faith is not a matter for the few, but for the many. According to church precepts, all those who are baptized are members of God's people. Each one of us is a child of God, a chosen daughter, a chosen son of God. In baptism, we receive not only this especially close relationship with God, but we are also qualified to speak to others of this relationship and to bear witness. We take part in the reign of Christ, in priesthood, and in the work of prophets.

You may be thinking, "That's all very well, but it's a bit much for me. And a bit too big." Good! It really is all too much and too big. If we did not feel a slight uncertainty and insecurity on this path, and some awe in the face of the magnitude of the task, we would soon be on the wrong path. In any case, today everyone seems to believe that they can "add their two cents" and say what they want. A slight insecurity about what I have to say in "holy" matters is good because it opens me up to the living God who sends us. It saves us from self-serving justice, false self-certainty, arrogance, and a dangerous over-identification with the religious. Only if I remain in constant wonder, like a child, can I bear witness in some way to the greatness of God.

So, on the one hand, it is good to become conscious of and expose oneself to the question: Can I do this? Can I answer competently, doing myself and the subject—God—justice? On the other hand, however, we may also gratefully receive the trust that Jesus gives us in this matter. Paul, who is seen as one of the Christian faith's greatest missionaries, is an example: without him, not one of us today would know anything about faith. But he entered the congregation a little "too late"—meaning after Jesus' death, unlike the twelve apostles. Before that, he had even persecuted the early Christians. Therefore, he sees himself as "one untimely born" and keeps emphasizing that he is an apostle in his letters (1 Cor 15:8; see also Rom 1:1, Gal 1:1, etc.). One can feel his self-doubt. And precisely these self-doubts open him up to the miracle that has occurred in Jesus' acceptance of Paul for who he is.

I don't need to be perfect and I don't need to understand everything before showing my faith or daring to open my mouth. What matters is whether, within me, I feel the impulse to show myself or say something in this moment.

## Together it can work

*...and sent them on ahead of him in pairs.*

As if Jesus had noticed people's uncertainty precisely in these matters, he sends the seventy out in pairs. That makes the mission easier. Jesus does not require anything superhuman from his disciples. Showing one's faith in a group is much easier. And Jesus does not mind that.

He has practical reasons for sending out the disciples in pairs: for one thing, in his culture, every testimony required confirmation by a second person to be valid. The second was meant to confirm and strengthen the claims of the first.

The community of two also offered some protection against those who might not agree with what one was saying. And finally, the small group prevented arrogance. It is always a little difficult to speak of "God" and "piety." If someone else is there who knows me, it forces me to stay authentic. Sometimes, we monks are invited to lectures or courses, and I notice that the witness I bear is much stronger when I don't go alone, but arrive in a small group of two or three. The different voices reflect different perspectives on faith, they give listeners the freedom to choose, and they show something of God's variety and richness, which can be expressed in so many ways. Faith does not "belong" to any one person; it belongs to all of us, and together we "belong" to Jesus (see 1 Cor 3:21–23). Jesus has given the gift of faith to all his disciples, and that gift becomes particularly "visible" when we are together: "Where two or three are gathered in my name, I am there among them" (Matt 18:20).

## Going where Jesus wants to go

*...to every town and place where he himself intended to go.*

The little afterthought that tells us that Jesus himself intends to go to the respective towns is showing us something crucial: in showing faith, what matters is always Christ, never us. I don't decide to whom I show my faith. Instead, what's developing here is the relationship between Jesus Christ and another person to whom *he* intends to go. We should therefore go to the people to whom Jesus wants to show his love and let Jesus' encounter with those people happen.

That puts a significant limit on our role as persons sent forth. We do not go because we feel like it—he sends us. We do not go where we want to—he determines where we are going. I find that thought incredibly relieving. It takes responsibility off my shoulders, and simultaneously gives the process beauty and dignity. I'm being entrusted with serving this encounter between God and Man. As persons sent forth, we are there for both the sender and the receiver. If we show our faith, we do it only to ease, enable, prompt, and prepare the communication between God and the other person. If everything goes well, the person we're speaking to can encounter the divine that is already within them or that wants to open up to them. So, we shouldn't stand in the way of this communication but contribute to it in whatever way we can. Doing that, we are fitting ourselves into a process that is greater than we are. If we see ourselves as the sender, we've done something wrong: not even Jesus sees himself in that role. He is sent by his Father: "The word that you hear is not mine, but is from the Father who sent me" (John 14:24). With these words, he places himself within a greater context.

## The Lord is the employer

*The harvest is plentiful, but the laborers are few.*

In this context, I keep encountering an apparently sensible argument that, on closer inspection, is very cynical: the number of priests may be decreasing—but the number of faithful is as well, so it all fits. No, it doesn't "all fit." Why not? Because that's just our human interpretation. We don't know whether God thinks this way. At least in this passage from Luke, Jesus' appraisal is very different. "The harvest is plentiful," he says. We don't get to decide whether the harvest is big or whether it's over. Some people are frustrated because many things are not going well for the Church. They see the decreasing numbers of the congregations and wonder whether the harvest is simply no longer as plentiful as it used to be.

"The harvest is plentiful," says Jesus. And adds, as if already in his time it was difficult to find people to commit to this kind of "work," "Ask the Lord of the harvest to send out laborers into his harvest." The Lord of the harvest is God, and Jesus himself feels sent out as one of the laborers. He sees the many needy, lonely people, those bowed down by hardship, the sick, the dying, the poor, the strangers...and wants to go to them. He wants to clothe the naked, heal the sick—through us. One could say that, in some sense, the problem isn't on the side of the receivers, and not on the side of the sender—that is, God—but on our side! Who wants to go into the vineyard and labor?

So, there is a very simple reason why we don't need to hide our faith: it doesn't belong to us at all! But in this sense, we're not allowed to hide it either, at least not when in our heart we hear—and to hear outside words strengthen our conscience in the conviction—that we should show ourselves or say something when the time is given. That's what is different from man-made convictions: it really is truly my decision how much I talk about my party affiliation or my vegetarianism. But when we're dealing with the divine, another dimension comes into play.

## An invitation to love

*Whatever house you enter, first say, "Peace to this house!"*

Jesus wants us to bring peace to every home, to every person—because that is what he himself wants to bring when he comes: "My peace I give to you" (John 14:27). *Shalom* was the greeting Jesus used—a blessing with which he wished peace, joy, and prosperity on those he encountered.

What matter to Jesus are first and foremost the people he encounters. He wants to let people feel the love and respect that he is constantly feeling from his Father. He remarks that the peace one wishes for people will remain with them if they are truly people "who share in peace," but will otherwise "return." In these words, he is showing how much he respects every person's freedom. Every person gets to decide whether or not they accept the blessing. This respect for the freedom of others is typical of Jesus' mission and should be the measure of ours, as well.

Jesus then goes on: "Cure the sick who are there, and say to them, 'The kingdom of God has come near to you.'" That's in line with the task he first articulated and deepens it: help people truly *experience* this love, this peace, this healing. Cure the sick! So, if we show our faith, it should be first through our actions, rather than our words. "Say to them: 'The kingdom of God has come near to you,'" comes second. What sense would it make to tell them this but refuse to help them experience it as well!

One of my favorite sentences on this topic comes from Francis of Assisi (1181–1226): "Preach the Gospel, and if necessary, use words." If we open up and show ourselves to others in faith, we should do it only in such a way that they later feel themselves more loved and accepted, more regarded and respected, a little more whole, joyful, and satisfied. From the beginning, Jesus' mission prohibits any kind of testifying that is aggressive or manipulative. That is not the purpose for which Jesus sends us out.

The Divine Word Missionary St. Joseph Freinademetz (1852–1908) put it plainly: "The only language all people understand is the language of love." (He would know—he traveled from South Tyrol to China as a missionary.) Love is an international and intercultural language. The heart of the other understands it immediately. Words are secondary and can even lead to misunderstandings.

The Missionary Benedictine Congregation of St. Ottilien, to which I belong, was founded in the nineteenth century for missionary work, and our confreres were sent primarily to Africa and Asia. In the twenty-first century, the theory and practice of missionary work are very different, of course—but how? In our last general chapter, we—African, Asian, American, and European confreres—asked ourselves this question. We were searching for a new common denominator and finally hit upon the formula: mission today means sharing God's love. That's an international project. Jesus' heart is full of this love, which is why he formulates it as the highest of all commandments: love God and love your neighbor as yourself (see Matt 22:37–39). This love extends beyond itself and wants to be handed on.

It's the same with young couples: the partners love each other so much that they want to pass this love on to their children. In passing it on, their love isn't diminished, but grows. Love wants to express itself. One of the happiest moments at a wedding occurs when the couple proudly shows their innermost conviction to the world and proclaims to everyone: We love each other! They want to call out to the entire world: I love this person! There is no better partner in the world!

Through the centuries, spreading love has become a sign of Christianity. Of course, Christians have not spread only love, and we need to be open about that, too, as I'll discuss later. But it's sensible and legitimate to point to the abundance of good that has happened in this world through the spread of Christianity. Heinrich Böll, one of twentieth-century German literature's greatest authors—who was not known for holding back when he criticized the Church—once said, "I would prefer even the very worst Christian world to the best heathen one, because in a Christian world there is room for those whom no heathen world has ever given room: for the crippled and ill, old and weak....I believe in Christ and I believe that millions of Christians on this earth can change the face of this world, and I recommend it to the contemplation and imagination of my contemporaries to imagine a world in which Christ had not existed."

Far more than seventy disciples, then, followed Jesus' call to share God's love and pass it on to all people. That call remains the model to this day. John Thomas Kattrukudiyil, the bishop of Ittanagar in northeast India, was once asked how he could account for the overwhelming growth of the Church in his diocese (over ten thousand new Christians per year). His answer: "Because we introduce God as the loving Father, and because people see how we love him." Love radiates and becomes active.

Everybody should have the opportunity of experiencing the joy of feeling themselves loved by God. It is a gift that one can't keep to oneself but must share with others. If we want to keep it only to ourselves, we become isolated, sterile, sick Christians.

## Traveling light

*Carry no purse, no bag, no sandals!*

Another one of Jesus' instructions relates to the "equipment" his disciples should bring with them. He recommends traveling light: "Take nothing for your journey, no staff, nor bag, nor bread, nor money—not even an extra tunic" (Luke 9:3). Why such radical simplicity? If it is true that Jesus sends us and intends to follow—if we are simply his messengers—then it's best to come without pomp. The less we push ourselves into the foreground the better, so that we don't block people's view of Jesus.

Jesus also recommends traveling light for reasons of credibility: we're most convincing when we come to people with nothing but ourselves and our faith. Jesus wants the message of God's reign to shine through us clear and undistorted. The more personal our testimony, the more effective it is. If, however, we come with trumpets and drums, with canons and guns, with checkbook and gifts, with entourage and accolades, people's attention will be drawn more to these "accessories" than to the essence of our message. "See, I am sending you out like lambs into the midst of wolves" (Luke 10:3). Our vulnerability is part of the same lack of baggage, because it is the same way in which Jesus himself spread the message of God's love.

If we're "barefoot," without money or supplies, when we encounter people, we are forced to encounter them truly as people. Bearing witness to faith is so simple: we're called to just be people. We don't need to do anything special or pretend to be anything special. We can just be ourselves, as we are. Because Jesus sent *me*. I don't need to worry about myself (or, in terms of Jesus' mission: I can eat what is set before me). The less pretense I bring to my encounter with others, the better.

Pope Francis reminds us vividly of this injunction to travel light: he chooses the less ostentatious cars, the simpler shoes. It's unbelievable what an effect that has. We want to see *people* when we see Christians, and that's not merely a question of perception, but of an attitude and way of life.

Furthermore, if I really want to engage with others, I need to be flexible. My thoughts and my hands need to be free so that I can serve others. I need to be able to take care more of the other person than of me. What use is great spiritual or practical equipment if I have no idea what the people I will meet really need? I should be open and ready to react to their individual needs. The Apostle Paul articulated that goal for himself in the phrase "become all things to all people" (1 Cor 9:22). Each piece of surplus baggage prevents me from engaging with others. In the West, the Church has lost much of its missionary power, but to this date has relinquished none of its financial holdings or real estate. If I have too many possessions, I become sluggish and uninterested in others. Property gives us security and stability. Jesus invites us, where possible, to forgo these, so that the witness we bear becomes more credible. At that point, we stop trusting our baggage and our preparation and start trusting him. Showing one's faith to others is a wonderful spiritual challenge to rely more on God than on oneself. Of course, letting go of everything is also connected with fear. But Jesus encourages us because he himself will take care of us. As he says later in the Gospel of Luke, "'When I sent you out without a purse, bag, or sandals, did you lack anything?' They said, 'No, not a thing'" (22:35). We might consider what we personally can give up—materially and in terms of attitude—so that our faith can become more visible to others.

# And what if I am turned away?

*Wipe the dust off your feet.*

The first journey that the seventy undertook must have been successful, at least according to the Gospel of Luke. Nevertheless, even before they set out, Jesus still prepares the disciples for the possibility that their mission may not be met with love: "But whenever you enter a town and they do not welcome you, go out into its streets and say, 'Even the dust of your town that clings to our feet, we wipe off in protest against you. Yet know this: the kingdom of God has come near'" (Luke 10:10–11).

If it is true that the message is not our private property and we have invested nothing material into the project other than ourselves—that is, if we have traveled light—it also becomes much easier to deal with if our testimony is rejected. In going, we shake hands. Shaking aids in the separation. In this case, Jesus recommends shaking the dust off one's feet. That is a strong gesture and was used in the ancient Orient, where it was less an expression of anger or vengefulness but rather of cleansing. Shake the dust off your feet—that is how you rid yourself of the things you didn't want to stay with you. Jesus does not say that we should react with displeasure or anger, or that we should reproach others. Each person's freedom is part of his message that we are spreading. That message remains, even where it is rejected. Therefore, Jesus here speaks of standing in the street and calling out the message once again: it does not depend on acceptance or rejection. Still, each person gets to decide for themselves whether they want to engage with the message or not.

One of Jesus' parables presents the occasional futility of human efforts as a practically natural fact (Matt 13:1–9): the sower must sow much more than he can expect to reap. In the same way, God is generous and has no problem offering his love. He "sows" more deeds and words than necessary to reap as many as possible. It is part of our earthly reality that not every person wants to or is able to follow—they may just not be ready yet.

Jesus' words help prevent our anger and frustration. In this context, I have learned a lot from the business and sales-people I met when I was still working in the publishing world. These professionals have learned to internalize a tolerance for frustration: they're pleased when they can sell a book, but they know that the book might also just lie unsold in a bookstore somewhere. Wiping the dust off one's feet and moving on. Sure, it's sad: "Whoever listens to you listens to me, and who-ever rejects you rejects me, and whoever rejects me rejects the one who sent me" (Luke 10:16). But for the moment, we've done all we can.

## It brings joy

*The seventy returned with joy....At that same hour Jesus rejoiced in the Holy Spirit and said, "I thank you, Father."*

The journey was joyous. The disciples were full of their experiences, and I can almost see them exchange stories, laugh-ing and proud. They were filled with encounters with the other people, were filled with the spirit of Jesus, literally inspired. They really were able to heal people and cast out demons. What Jesus foretold, even though it seemed unimaginable, has become truth: "The one who believes in me will also do the works that I do and, in fact, will do greater works than these" (John 14:12). Who'd have thought it? Being fascinated by Jesus, that is one thing, but being capable of making the message of God's love effective, just like Jesus himself did, that is a miracle.

It appears Jesus was waiting for these disciples. He is not one to send people off on a mission and then forget about them or lose interest, as often happens in a job: once a task has been delegated, no one cares about it anymore. It's good to know that Jesus himself waits for us and wants to know how we have fared. Jesus is our "home base," as it were—we can always return to him. There is always someone home because Jesus is always there for us, a person we can simply tell what we have experienced, a person with whom we can share our joy.

We do this far too rarely. Since religion is taboo and spirituality is a private matter, we don't share our experiences with others enough. That means we lose out not just on others' experience and knowledge but also on a great deal of joy. But Jesus is interested. He reacts lovingly to the enthusiastic tales. First, he confirms the "successes" of his disciples: Yes, "I watched Satan fall from heaven like a flash of lightning" (Luke 10:18). Even from a distance, he has perceived what happened to the disciples and what they have accomplished. Their positive experiences are not figments of their imagination. Their joy is well founded.

After this confirmation, however, Jesus adds something else: "Nevertheless, do not rejoice at this, that the spirits submit to you, but rejoice that your names are written in heaven" (Luke 10:20). Does Jesus want to immediately dampen his disciples' joy? No, but he takes the opportunity to teach them something more: the "successful" missionary is in danger of becoming drunk with success and attributing the things of which he is capable to himself. He is in danger of forgetting that he has been "successful" only because Jesus has sent him, because Jesus trusted him, because it was Jesus himself who intended to go to the people. Jesus worked the miracle. There is no reason for the disciples to get above themselves—quite the opposite:

much of the evil in the history of Christian missions comes precisely from the fact that the missionaries forgot that they are
"only" *sent* by God, and that they are not God themselves.
Nevertheless, it is cause for joy that such unbelievable closeness
can arise between the disciples and God (their names are written down by God).

At this point, the evangelist Luke inserts the so-called
rejoicing of Jesus: "I thank you, Father, Lord of heaven and
earth, because you have hidden these things from the wise and
the intelligent and have revealed them to infants" (Luke 10:21).
Thereafter, we read that he turned back to the disciples and
"said to them privately..." (v. 23). The last sentence makes clear
that Jesus hides his jubilation from the disciples. Possibly, he
does not want to inflame their pride.

This story is uplifting in that it tells us how much Jesus
himself is glad that the disciples have done so well. His message
has resonated with people, and the disciples have profited from
it, too. All is well. There are only a few moments in the Gospels
in which Jesus shows true emotion. But here, we can practically
hear him shout a happy "Yes! It worked!"—and this enthusiasm
turns into praise of God—"I thank you, Father,"—since everything originated with the Father.

I once asked an old missionary, who had spent over fifty
years living and praying with people in the Tanzanian bush-
lands, "What was your most joyous experience so far?" He told
the following story: "Once, in our congregation in Nyangao, we
held a marriage seminar. One hundred fifty couples had come.
We were together for two days, and at the end we held a service
which finished with a dance of joy. I will never forget that." Joy
and gratitude for the love that one receives from God—those
are the true characteristics of mission. When we talk about
passing on the faith these days, we often do so in an undertone

of frustration or worried reticence. But it is a thing of joy! As Christians, as parents, grandparents, religious teachers— wherever we stand, the first thing we should share with others is joy. *Gospel* means "glad tidings."

## GOD LOVES REVEALING HIMSELF

Being open about ourselves and our faith can sometimes be a real journey. Even though, in our everyday lives, it can happen in fractions of a second, we are, nevertheless, entrusted with an entire inner journey in that time. The reason is that in bearing witness, we come very close to the "nature" of God. In that process, we are invited to open ourselves entirely to him and to those things he wants to do through us. But God's nature is to spread himself into the world, to give himself as a gift. God is love. And love cannot remain alone. It is creative—so God created the world, in his own image. God reveals himself in creation. Today, so many people sense that nature and creation are expressions of the divine. Revealing himself in creation gives God joy—and it gives us joy to see God in it.

But that, we believe, wasn't enough for God: he wanted to reveal himself directly, in his very nature. He personally wanted to reveal himself—undisguised, visible to all people, vulnerable, tangible—and so his son was born. With no purse, no bag, no sandals. And again, God does not love hiding himself. Instead, he reveals himself in Jesus. If we look into Jesus' eyes, we see God. When we see his actions, we recognize God. In listening to his words, we hear God.

God doesn't want to keep his divinity to himself. He wants to share it. He is ultimately inclusive, one might say that he wants all to have life, divine life, in abundance (see John 10:10). God is radiating love. That is what we express when we speak of the triune God: God is not a monolith, but three persons connected with one another in love. The theology of the trinity developed by St. Augustine refers to God's "missions," the *missiones dei*.[1] In other words, Jesus Christ, the Son of God, proceeds from the Father, he is "sent out" from him, just like the Holy Spirit. From a Christian viewpoint, God's nature contains "missions." God goes out of himself, he flows outward, the Son from the Father and the Holy Spirit from the Father and the Son. That is the theological center of missionary work. Because God is missionary—that is, God did not want to remain with himself, but went outside of himself, opened himself up to others—we, too, are invited to resonate with this divine dynamic, to go outside ourselves and reveal our true selves.

That thought gives me joy: through my own humble means, I can participate in the divine dynamic. I also find the thought relieving, because the task is a larger one for which God has the final responsibility. My only responsibility is to open myself to him. I can show myself as a person, without hiding, just as God made me, because I mirror something of his beauty, his truth, his goodness.

## DOUBTING IS OKAY

We know from experience that it isn't always that simple. First, one doesn't always feel immediately close to God throughout the course of a normal day. Second, one just wants to be authentic. For example, if I teach religion, the only things I can still teach children and students today are the things I really believe myself. Anything I have not understood or experienced, everything about the Christian faith that is of no use to me—the things that I personally don't live or the teachings I don't follow—in all those things, no one is going to believe me anyway.

When we reveal ourselves, we want to reveal ourselves as we are, especially in religious matters. We do not want to pretend, to play at something false. I can touch others only if I'm authentic, if I'm my true self. Any kind of pretense or hypocrisy scares people away rather than draws them toward me. Only when I truly stand behind the things I bear witness to is my testimony honest and compelling. This standard of authenticity, however, can hide a temptation as well. After all, authenticity means that I am in accord with myself—but do I always know who I am? When have I ever known that with complete accuracy? And when can I be 100 percent certain of what I believe? Perfectionism can lead us to hide forever, since we can never be *completely* certain.

In this regard, we can learn a great deal from the apostle Thomas. He wanted complete certainty as well. The other disciples told him that Jesus is risen, he lives! They showed themselves to him in their faith. But Thomas didn't trust them. He wanted to see and experience it for himself, wanted to touch the hand of Jesus to be completely sure. Jesus respects his wish and returns to his disciples one week after his first appearance. He shows Thomas the wounds on his hands and feet, and Thomas falls to his knees, believes, and proclaims, "My Lord and my God!" (John 20:28).

What helps Thomas believe? It is that Jesus shows him his wounds, that Jesus shows his vulnerability to Thomas. The disciples probably ran to Thomas full of enthusiasm. They were completely sure of Jesus, and certainly authentic as well—but they were not convincing. Thomas may have thought, "Are they being carried away by wishful thinking? I want to be sure." Jesus answers this need. The thing that finally convinces Thomas is Jesus showing his wounds.

This is a model of bearing witness: sometimes it's better to show one's religious convictions in all their brokenness and incompleteness than to arrive on the scene with titanic conviction. For example, we can let our doubts shine through by saying things such as "I'm not sure, but I feel that..."; "I believe that..., but I could easily be wrong, of course"; "I used to see it that way, but now I feel this..."; or even "I can't give a good reason, but I believe...." An even more specific example: "In the Old Testament, God enjoins us to keep the Sabbath day holy, and the Church wants us to attend services every Sunday. I must admit that I don't always go. Sometimes I can't attend, but sometimes I'm simply too lazy. But when I do go, I feel better. And I find it to be a good and important thing."

If we include doubting Thomas in our testimony, we are more convincing than if we appear above all doubts. If, like Jesus, we show our vulnerability, his love can more easily reach us.

But it is part of our vulnerability that, in bearing witness, we continuously depend on others. For example, that means this: Is it really such a dreadful thing if I say that I believe or do one thing or another simply because the Church says so? Isn't it completely fine if I join a community of billions and figure that they can't all be completely crazy? If we feel the need to believe and justify our whole faith from within ourselves, there isn't that much faith left. That gets overwhelming. Instead, I am invited to move gradually from "learned" to "lived" faith over the course of my life. The community of the faithful can help me in this.

Before sending them out, Jesus does not ask his disciples, Have you understood everything? Do you live everything exactly as you will proclaim it? Do you stand behind it completely? Because you can bear witness of me only if you are completely authentic!

Instead, he sends along a second disciple for support. This second disciple, one could say, stands in for the community of the faithful. It is enough for Jesus that he himself sends us out. It is not us who make our testimony true; that is his role. It is his truth. Br. Roger (1915–2005), the founder of Taizé, once advised, "Live the part of the gospel you have understood—however little that may be. But live it!" For those who have come to see accordance with Church teaching—with the community of the faithful—as important, here, too, nothing needs to be perfect. Start with what you believe in. In my life, I often didn't really understand certain articles of faith or even moral teachings of the Church for years, or simply couldn't categorize them. I also had difficulty living them—until one day I happened upon the experience that showed me: Hey, what the Church teaches is exactly right!

St. Paul the Apostle says,

Love never ends. But as for prophecies, they will come to an end; as for tongues, they will cease; as for knowledge, it will come to an end. For we know only in part, and we prophesy only in part; but when the complete comes, the partial will come to an end. When I was a child, I spoke like a child, I thought like a child, I reasoned like a child; when I became an adult, I put an end to childish ways. For now we see in a mirror, dimly, but then we will see face to face. Now I know only in part; then I will know fully, even as I have been fully known. And now faith, hope, and love abide, these three; and the greatest of these is love. (1 Cor 13:8–13)

I do not need to wait for my knowledge of the divine to be complete before I begin to tell of it. For my whole life, I will remain one who learns and grows; I am allowed to move from insight to insight, and however incomplete or fragmentary my insights are, I am even now allowed to bear witness if my testimony is borne by hope and love.

2

# BEFORE SETTING OUT

Maybe you have already started to feel a growing desire to express your faith outwardly. It's a spiritual path on which we can grow and come closer to our divine center. But before we "let ourselves loose on others," we should take three principles to heart, which I recommend to you:

Begin your mission in prayer and silence.

First apply your message to yourself.

Have courage!

## BEGIN IN PRAYER AND SILENCE

Before Jesus begins to work in public, he retreats to the desert. It is the Holy Spirit that leads him there. This time spent in solitude, silence, and prayer is important in preparation for his eventual preaching and healing. But even during the active period of his life, Jesus keeps returning to solitude: "Jesus departed with his disciples to the sea" (Mark 3:7); "Now when Jesus heard this, he withdrew from there in a boat to a deserted place by himself" (Matt 14:13); "In the morning, while it was still very dark, he got up and went out to a deserted place, and there he prayed" (Mark 1:35). We encounter these remarks so often in the gospel that they almost sound like a pattern—and perhaps the evangelists provided some editorial help, as well. But what's certain is that Jesus sought not only closeness with others but also closeness to God in the absence of others.

In this respect, Jesus' mission seems fundamentally different from all other possible "missions" that a company, organization, or individual might have: Jesus' mission comes out of silence and leads back to silence and prayer—because prayer is a special place of closeness to God. If our testimony isn't supported by this element of silence, of respect, of love, and of the living dialogue with God, we are more like "a noisy gong or a clanging cymbal" (1 Cor 13:1). I may draw attention to myself, but I also have nothing to communicate.

Several years ago, I had the opportunity of getting to know a group that, in their way of bearing witness, compelled and touched me deeply: the consecrated women of the international Verbum Dei Missionary Fraternity. It's hard to imagine a life that is more active, more united in solidarity, or closer to people. But each Wednesday, all women retreat to do one thing and one thing only: be with Jesus in silence, to pray, share their faith with one another, and recollect themselves. And once a year, each sister engages in a full month of silent retreat. They assured me that this is necessary not only for collecting ideas for more sermons and lectures, but also to reorient themselves toward him who sends them.

Silence and prayer protect us when we speak about God and our faith. They save us from the violence that might be within our words or deeds, from the temptation of manipulation, and from becoming ingratiating or vain.

Monasteries today have a great significance, and one reason for that may be that the monks and nuns who inhabit them try to let everything they do originate in prayer. People not only see that, they feel it as well. In our hectic lives, we don't need another person who is overfilled with their own activism and brushes past us superficially. We want to encounter people who draw on depth, even contemplation. "For while gentle silence enveloped all things, / and night in its swift course was now half gone, / your all-powerful word leaped from heaven, from the royal throne" (Wis 18:14–15). This text from the Old Testament is sung by monks in their Gregorian chants for Christmas. The silence of Christmas Eve is the moment in which God goes outside himself, shows himself, "leaps down" from his throne, and becomes man. Jesus, the Word of God, proceeds from silence. Our words and deeds should do the same.

This mysterious "procession" of the Son of God from the Father is at the beginning of any good news we bring. If we aren't in touch with this mystery—which we can only reach in silence and prayer—we will always be telling more of ourselves than of God. Recognizing that by passing on our faith, we are partaking in the work of God himself, that realization is the only thing that can protect us from the power of our private motivations and interests. Jesus himself is the "mission" of God. Before we succumb to all kinds of activism, we should first connect with him in prayer and listen to where he wants to send us. We will not add anything special to his mission, only serve it.

In 1927, Pope Pius XI named the Jesuit Francis Xavier (1506–52) and the Carmelite nun Thérèse of Lisieux (1873–97) patron saints of the missions. This elevation of "Little Thérèse" to a co-patron has always seemed provocative to me: while Xavier quite obviously did significant mission work, going as far as India and Japan, this young woman never left her monastery. How could one call her a missionary? Why should she of all people be a co-patron of world missions? Maybe precisely because she prayed for missionaries locally, partaking herself in that mysterious dynamic that radiates outward from God in prayer and silence. By doing this, she may have made a much greater contribution than we think.

Silence is the best way to learn the skill of listening. To bear witness, you first have to listen: What does my conscience say within me? What is the truth that I should speak? Bearing witness is a wonderful way to get to know oneself and one's innermost soul better. St. Benedict begins his rule with these words: "Listen carefully, my son, my daughter, to the master's instructions, and attend to them with the ear of your heart."[1] We often don't know who we really are until we attend to ourselves and by doing so show ourselves to the world.

But listening is also the best way to encounter others in respect and love—otherwise, what follows is not a dialogue but a monologue. In listening, I can perceive the other fully and whole; together we can listen for the impulses of the divine that want to reveal themselves in the other person.

If we take more time for that silence, we are already doing good, and not just for ourselves. If we can incorporate little rituals into our everyday life that connect us with our divine center, we will become infectious for others. If we live an active life of prayer, maybe in the evenings or in the mornings, in little bursts, in traditional prayer formulas, or in free prayer, we're already doing good for others and passing on our faith.

## MISSIONIZE YOURSELF FIRST

In the earlier section, "Doubting Is Okay," we were encouraged to show our faith, even if it is flawed. It's important to relieve some of the pressure we may put on ourselves, otherwise we'll never have the courage or the confidence to bear witness, or our testimony will become so "correct" that we can't stand it.

But that doesn't detract from the fact that we're supposed to live the things that we want to show in our faith. Those who preach water while drinking wine will be unlikely to find much of an audience. John advises, "Let us love, not in word or speech, but in truth and action" (1 John 3:18). Authenticity is an important criterion for our missionary work. Those who don't at least attempt to practice what they preach are not convincing and will produce alienation and ridicule rather than approval.

What specifically does that mean? It means that I should always be the first addressee of the witness I bear. If I am testifying to love but do not act lovingly, that is of no use to me or to anyone else—it has no effect. If I speak hopelessly of hope, I will reach no one. If I speak of joy—to me this is the most obvious case—but am not joyous and at peace, I will not be compelling. If, however, I have first converted myself, that already has a positive effect that will radiate outward without my having to do very much. To convince John and Simon to follow him, Jesus simply shows them where and how he lives (see John 1:39). That silent missionizing is often the most effective. Loud preachers who thunder at their listeners with utter conviction often turn out later to be people who are completely subject to their weaknesses and have lived lives that are morally questionable. However, those who speak softly may also be hypocrites.

I am the first addressee of my testimony. If I open myself to the things I am proclaiming, I need not have fully understood them or even put them fully into practice—but I should let God work in me. I often notice that about my own sermons: while I'm preparing, I try to let the good news that I'm preaching work in my own life. If it is a sermon about the blessedness of the poor, I try to believe actively in this promise and to discover the beauty and grace of "having less" in my life. Or I try to reach out to the poor and help them in practical ways. If I'm going to preach about service, I can do so even without necessarily being the best servant because what my listeners feel is whether I apply this message to myself, whether I, too, am working on it.

After all, the message does not *belong* to me. It would be an illusion to think that I could ever "possess" it. It is *directed toward* me. I am the first addressee of my missionary work. This is true not only on the level of successful communication but is also deeply rooted in theology. Christianity begins with change. Jesus went to the river Jordan and followed John the Baptist's call to repent. When he himself began to preach, his first message was: "Repent, and believe in the good news" (Mark 1:15). Repentance has thus been a part of Christianity from the very beginning: one first had to want to change one's life, to live from God in deed, and only then was one baptized. One left military service, stopped having that affair, gave half of one's wealth to the poor, stopped drinking, made peace with one's neighbors—only then did one become a Christian. These days, we often forget that part. If we have the courage to testify more to our faith, that might function as encouragement to work more on ourselves, too, so that our actions may be as close as possible to our beliefs.

If I stop repenting and changing—even long after my first repentance or baptism—my deeds will be hollow. But if I honestly and humbly continue to work on change, then the message itself (rather than me) will resonate through me. What people see becomes what the message is doing to me, how it is working on me and transforming me. In his encyclical *Redemptoris Missio*, Pope John Paul II said, "The true missionary is the saint." Mission is a spiritual occurrence.

## HAVE COURAGE!

Start in silence, persevere along your own spiritual path, and then pay attention to where a person or situation "calls" you to go outside of yourself by doing or showing something. This action of going outside of yourself will require courage.

Often, what prevents us from proclaiming our faith is a slight fear—an understandable one since we are making ourselves vulnerable in showing our faith. How can we deal with this fear sensibly?

Expressed simply, there are two kinds of fear. One is a warning: a mountain climber looks down, and his fear tells him, "Be careful!" This fear protects us and has an important function for our survival. The other kind of fear is "threshold anxiety." It happens naturally when we face something new, for example, as a child on the first day of school, as a student before graduation, as a woman before the birth of her child, or as a performer before walking onstage. It is a fear that—unlike the previous one—*invites* us to walk forward through the fear. This fear does not want to warn us off: don't complete school, don't go onstage, don't have children! Instead, it helps us muster the necessary adrenaline for mastering what is ahead of us.

When we show our faith, we're leaving our comfort zone and walking toward a deep encounter with others. It's completely understandable to feel slight trepidation in the face of that encounter.

In such situations, Antonia Werr (1813–68), the founder of the Franciscan Servants (now a congregation spanning the world), used to tell herself, "Trust in Him, He guides You, He leads You: have courage!" A confrere of mine likes to say, "Have no fear, God is good!" After all, whom am I really trying to encounter in my missionary work? I am searching for God, for Christ in my fellow beings. Is there anything more beautiful? So, have no fear of Christ! If, instead, I happen to meet the "demons," the Lord will give me the necessary strength for that situation as well since he was the one to send me. Maybe it was to counter this fear that, when sending out his disciples, Jesus said, "See, I am sending you out like lambs into the midst of wolves" (Luke 10:3). He was affirming that doing this can be risky.

Paul the missionary says, "For God did not give us a spirit of cowardice, but rather a spirit of power and of love and of self-discipline" (2 Tim 1:7). Cowardice is not the fruit of the Holy Spirit. They say that the Bible contains the sentence "Do not be afraid" 365 times—once for each day of the year. The central message of the Old Testament is this: You, Israel, have a God who has made a covenant with you. And the New Testament message: You, humanity, have a God whom you can call "*Abba*," Father, and who in Christ has forgiven all your missteps and who has raised his good reign in your midst. So why be afraid? Indeed, early Christians felt fear to be something typically heathen. As Christians, we can conquer fear by the Holy Spirit.

I'm not advertising some sort of daredevil idea of "Holy War." But I am talking about the courage that grows in us from our faith. It does no harm here to be reminded of "The Little World of Don Camillo," who when at a loss prayed to God and abdicated responsibility to him, saying something like, "Lord, you got me into this situation, now give me the courage for it."

Consider the following everyday examples: A friend of mine plays in a band that performs mainly Christian music. He tells me that what he would really like is for them to start rehearsals by praying together, but he is worried that the suggestion will sound overbearing. He might suggest, "I would like to start the rehearsal with a prayer. It would do me good. Can we try it? I don't want to sound pious or arrogant, but it really would do me good."

I have often wondered whether to make the sign of the cross before eating in a place other than my monastery, like a restaurant, for example. But why not? With God, I can have the courage to do so. I have gotten into the habit, in those moments, of praying not just for me but for everyone in the room silently. There has never been a problem.

So, there aren't as many "wolves" out there as one might think. How one deals with the ones that do exist is another topic to which we will return later.

The Church knows the courage that bearing witness requires. In his encyclical *Redemptoris Missio*, John Paul II writes about "missionary spirituality": "An example of this is found with the apostles during the Master's public life. Despite their love for him and their generous response to his call, they proved to be incapable of understanding his words and reluctant to follow him along the path of suffering and humiliation. The Spirit transformed them into courageous witnesses to Christ and enlightened heralds of his word. It was the Spirit himself who guided them along the difficult and new paths of mission" (no. 87). Pope Francis, in turn, encourages youth with the words of Christ: "I have said this to you, so that in me you may have peace. In the world you face persecution. But take courage; I have conquered the world!" (John 16:33).

## FIND YOUR OWN WAYS OF PROCLAIMING YOUR FAITH

Luckily, God did not create us all the same. The ways in which we talk about faith or bear witness are as different as our personalities. There is no norm; each one of us is invited to do so in our own way.

The Myers-Briggs personality type indicator can help us reflect on our preferred style.[2] It was developed based on C. G. Jung's personality typology and is now mostly used in coaching and the business sector. Speaking generally, it distinguishes between introverted and extroverted people. An extroverted person, on the one hand, is energized by time they spend interacting with others: they are "recharged." But it is draining for extroverts to be on their own. Introverts, on the other hand, draw energy from time spent by themselves. Being around too many people or being around others for too long is strenuous. In Western societies, extroverts have a slight edge because they tend to be the ideal type.[3] When it comes to showing faith or talking about personal questions in general, there is, of course, a significant difference between being an introvert or an extrovert. Extroverts find it easy to step out of themselves. Introverts, however, need to cross an internal threshold. Finding that the Bible contains models for both forms of bearing witness was an important and touching discovery for me. Personally, I am more of an introvert, but look and see what model works better for you:

> Do not fear what they fear, and do not be intimidated, but in your hearts sanctify Christ as Lord. Always be ready to make your defense to anyone who demands from you an accounting for the hope that is in you; yet do it with gentleness and reverence. Keep your conscience clear. (1 Pet 3:14–16)

Here, the initiative for bearing witness does not come from the missionary but from the person who is seeking—so we should be ready to answer. We shouldn't run around talking about faith constantly, whether anyone wants to listen or not. But in the case where someone asks, we should speak honestly. Being "always ready," nevertheless, requires a certain amount of activity. We should expect someone to ask, and we should wonder at their question. We should not seek to avoid this moment or fail to answer. We should sanctify Christ within our hearts, that is, we should always keep in touch with him privately.

Today, this model is probably the most generally appropriate. It has a gentleness to it. I am preparing myself for the unlikely event. I do not impose on others, am not manipulative, and certainly never violent. I aim to bear witness "humbly," not loudly, not proudly, and not with too much self-certainty. As already noted, these days, when someone is convinced of something 150 percent, we tend to recoil. This may be a reaction to the ideologies of the twentieth century (national socialism, fascism, communism). We've been through enough bad experiences. But simple, human answers to questions of faith, answers born of experience—these surely continue to have the opportunity of being heard.

The second model can be found close to the end of the Gospel of Matthew, and has been the defining force behind missionary work for the last few centuries:

> And Jesus came and said to them, "All authority in heaven and on earth has been given to me. Go therefore and make disciples of all nations, baptizing them in the name of the Father and of the Son and of the Holy Spirit, and teaching them to obey everything that I have commanded you. And remember, I am with you always, to the end of the age." (Matt 28:18–20)

Here, the missionary actively sets out to do work, following a call to action. The missionary doesn't wait to be approached but speaks out of oneself—one doesn't just speak, one acts as well. And one doesn't act in just any way: he or she baptizes. And one doesn't baptize in just any way: he or she baptizes in the name of the "Father and of the Son and of the Holy Spirit." This is a directed form of missionary work. Actively approaching people on questions of faith is practiced less often today than it once was. We don't want to be associated with mass baptisms or forced conversions. But Jesus' mission contains immense potential for us: he encourages us to reach out actively to others. That can be especially helpful if no one asks about faith anymore. If the person across from us has stopped looking altogether or has no sense of the religious, how can he or she ask us questions of faith? Then I am invited to start a conversation. If I do so with love and respect, it can help others discover a new dimension in their lives.

As an introvert, I am encouraged by "Do not fear...and do not be intimidated" from the Epistle of Peter. Yet, I am also strengthened by the energy contained in Jesus' words from the Gospel of Matthew: "Go therefore and make disciples of all nations, baptizing them...and teaching them to obey everything that I have commanded you!"

One thing I particularly need to learn is to go outside of myself. Are we not too complacent in our testimony anyway? In that case, the exhortation from Matthew 28 can invigorate us. After all, they are the closing words of the first Gospel in the New Testament.

For extroverts, however, the first model can encourage us: Don't jump the gun! Wait until you are really needed and welcome. That's true in general—and particularly in matters of faith. But the sort of person I am is not the only criterion. Above all, we should let ourselves be guided by the person across from us and their needs. We should always ask ourselves, What is good for this individual person? Do they want to be addressed at all? Or should I wait for them to bring up the topic?

3

# UNDERSTANDING "MISSION"

So far, I have used the word *mission* sparingly because it is such a loaded and misunderstood term. There is a lengthy list of reasons why it is difficult to use the term in a religious sense. We may associate it with intolerance, colonization, and the destruction of culture.[1] It can recall the crusades and forced conversions and baptisms. It is shameful and sad that church leaders themselves are mostly responsible for this poisoning of the term, which shares the fate of other phrases that can no longer be used because they were misused by others—such as "Strength through Joy"[2] or "Big Brother." Interestingly, *mission* is not equally "charred" in all languages. For example, *mission* in English is far less loaded than it is in German. In a nonreligious sense, any company can have its mission statement, as can an individual. My hope is that a new way of bearing witness can reopen the closed doors of the religious sentiment in the use of the term.

It's not only large parts of society but also the Church that has some difficulty with the term—at least in the case of the Catholic Church. The Second Vatican Council (1962–65) finally examined those unholy periods in church history and the dark aspects of its own theology and answered for them. The declaration *Nostra Aetate* was itself an attempt to address accusations of intolerance by unequivocally stating that salvation can be found outside the Church as well, and that traces of the divine are visible in all persons and religions.[3] This made obsolete the

Church's previous claim to absoluteness. And in the last fifty years, there has been no serious or far-reaching attempt to roll back this development. That is because the Church has learned its lesson. The process is irreversible—both in theory and in practice. I'm not aware of any cases since in which the Church has intolerantly used violence toward those of other faiths.

The criticism of cultural destructiveness was met with the idea of inculturation, which is central to post-Vatican II missionary theology. It means, simply, that Christian faith excludes the destruction of the encountered cultures and instead seeks to inculturate itself into the respective context. The gospel is meant to illuminate the beauty and dignity of all cultures. I could give many examples of the ways in which this idea is lived, including our own congregation of Benedictine missionaries in Africa, Asia, and other continents.

So, the Second Vatican Council achieved an urgently needed cleansing and reorientation—but this only serves to highlight the almost tragic part of this new idea: we became slightly scared of talking about faith at all, which is understandable in the context of our history. That meant that my own religious socialization was shaped by the conviction articulated in the following line from a German song: "Stop that missionizing; the victory is peace!" How often I sang that as a teenager! And how sad that I did, because in the end missionizing and making peace are not opposites but the very same thing: Jesus wants us to first say, "Shalom, peace!" to others. But in those years, *not* proclaiming one's faith was practically a mark of having the "right" spirituality. Many members of religious orders stopped wearing their habits as a sign of inculturation into modern society.

A personal experience may illustrate what I mean. As a novice in my Benedictine abbey, I helped out with youth courses.

The young people around me knew me as a monk, dressed in my black habit. Then, when I began to study outside the monastery, at the university, I felt that it would be good to go to class in the same habit, because that was how my peers knew me from the monastery. What can I say? It was the 1980s, and so I did not even manage a full year. I got many strange looks, as if I were some "ultraconservative," which I most definitely wasn't. All I had wanted was to be authentic. In Western countries, in contrast to many other places in the world, we can often no longer recognize priests or the members of religious orders when they are among the public. But as Vatican II became less immediate history, the popes, beginning with Paul VI, began to remind us of our duty to mission. John Paul II introduced the term "new evangelization" to refer to the revival of faith in areas that had already been Christian. He also embodied the new missionary spirit. No pope before him had visited so many countries, and in each, he kissed the ground of the place before he even opened his lips. Even the shy Benedict XVI held a synod dedicated exclusively to mission and the new evangelization (December 27, 2012). These efforts, however, resonated only poorly in the German church.

Germany underwent a fundamental change in 1989. When the Berlin Wall fell, the number of people who had become strangers to faith multiplied overnight. And yet there was no impulse in churches to say, "Let's actively offer our faith!" That hesitancy was understandable, given that East Germans were fed up with any kind of imposed belief system. But there was also a kind of missionary paralysis. One happy exception was the open letter written by Reinhard Wanke, the archbishop of Erfurt, titled "Time to Sow: Being a Missionary Church."[4] In general, however, the disappearance of the term *mission* had led to the disappearance of the concept itself.

When churches realized this and simultaneously saw that they would soon go extinct if they did not actively spread the faith, there was an effort to add a missionary dimension to nearly everything. But while talking about "missionary pastoral care" and "missionary congregation development" in drawn-out, coffee-and-cake get-togethers, the fact that mission has always meant going beyond one's own horizons and outside one's comfort zone was largely forgotten.

## TRANSCENDING BOUNDARIES
### Approaching and expanding one's horizons

I was once invited to address the graduating class of a vocational school. The school was only a few miles from our monastery. Since I was used to giving lectures in our monastery's guesthouse, I had a few building blocks for a lecture ready. But as soon as I entered the classroom, I felt that it would never work! Nothing of what I had prepared would be usable since most students came from an immigrant background and, I suspected, most of them were Muslim. I knew immediately that I would have to change the entire talk, and started off, at random, with Old Testament stories, hoping that their style would be most accessible to these young people. It worked! I was glad—but that little "culture shock" has stayed with me. Truthfully, I am ashamed that I hadn't taken the time beforehand to find out about my audience. I'm ashamed of this kind of arrogance that doesn't look past the end of one's own nose.

To reach these young people, I had to leave my culture, my circle, my "world"; I had to give up my stories and words. I had to step outside myself and trust entirely the things that wanted to reveal themselves in the encounter. Essentially, any conversation about faith and the meaning of life is a way of going beyond one's own borders. While I stay in my own boundaries, I cannot form any relationships. I need to go on a journey into the other person's "world."[5] Since, in this case, we are talking about God, the transcendental—meaning the one who goes above and beyond other things and beings, who crosses boundaries—I can only get in touch with him, and thus also with the person across from me, if I can cross this boundary within myself.

Jesus was in a similar position. Once, when he left his homeland and traveled to the coastal region near Sidon and Tyre, a local woman whose daughter was very sick came to him and began to shout,

> "Have mercy on me, Lord, Son of David; my daughter is tormented by a demon." But he did not answer her at all. And his disciples came and urged him, saying, "Send her away, for she keeps shouting after us." He answered, "I was sent only to the lost sheep of the house of Israel." But she came and knelt before him, saying, "Lord, help me." He answered, "It is not fair to take the children's food and throw it to the dogs." She said, "Yes, Lord, yet even the dogs eat the crumbs that fall from their masters' table." Then Jesus answered her, "Woman, great is your faith! Let it be done for you as you wish." And her daughter was healed instantly. (Matt 15:22-28)

Jesus' reaction was harsh and seems practically small-minded, bigoted even. He may have been in "vacation mode": no healing today, come back during regular business hours. It's more likely that he simply took the mission to his people, his compatriots and fellow faithful, very seriously. He knew that he did not have much time, and he could not do everything for everyone. What we can see here is how even Jesus had to let himself be corrected in his mission—corrected by the very people he encountered.

The woman's reaction was profound. With humor and humility, she gave herself a place in Jesus' limited attitude and precisely through that ensured that he listened closely. Biblical scholars generally consider that this is the point at which Jesus first understood his mission as being universal. Struck by the dignity and suffering of this woman, he realized that his message could not be confined to Israel.

When we bear witness, therefore, we are entering the richly blessed danger area of growing beyond ourselves. We are leaving our comfort zone and expanding our horizons. This openness to going to our boundaries and crossing them is the only way to resist the temptations of arrogance and manipulation.

If we step out of ourselves in this way, we become capable of going where others no longer dare go: the outer margins of society. That's why Jesus turned to the underprivileged and the outcast: he was not afraid of closeness to lepers, had unusually frequent connections with women (who were then second-class citizens), accepted dinner invitations from collaborators with the Roman occupiers, and shared meals with prostitutes. The Jesuits, an order whose members seek to follow in Jesus' footsteps and who have a particularly strong missionary outlook, have therefore reformulated the term *mission* for themselves as "being sent to the boundaries."[6]

Missionaries cross borders and boundaries: cultural, national, existential, social, and linguistic ones. This approach understands missionaries as people who walk in no-man's-land, both within society and within their own church. The Apostle Paul, early Christianity's quintessential missionary, constantly walked these borders, and in these encounters with people of non-Jewish origins and in prayer he recognized that the "heathens" should not be coerced into the Jewish ritual of circumcision if they wanted to become Christians.[7] Conversion itself became their "circumcision." When the subject was discussed with the established Christians in Jerusalem—with Jacob, Peter, and John, who in Paul's Epistle to the Galatians were termed the "acknowledged pillars"—Paul's view finally carries the day. The church renews itself from its borders inward.

In the Council of Cardinals, Pope Francis, who advocates a stronger decentralization of the Church in the spirit of the new evangelization, made the following observation: "Evangelizing implies apostolic zeal. Evangelizing presupposes in the Church the *parrhesia* ['free-speaking'] of coming out from itself. The Church is called to come out from itself and to go to the peripheries, not only geographical, but also existential: those of the mystery of sin, of suffering, of injustice, those of ignorance and of the absence of faith, those of thought, those of every form of misery."

Today, we engage in all sorts of diversions. We're looking for that "kick" that brings us into contact with energies that can't be called up anymore in our everyday lives. That might explain the sports that "push you to the edge," whether it be a marathon or bungee jumping. I suggest a different alternative: Why not talk about faith with your neighbor? It should give you at least a hint of danger.

## Jesus treasures strangers

Jesus was certainly a man with a keen sense of humor, but he became very serious when he started talking about the judgment of God. As categories that may open up his beloved Father's realm, he listed visiting the sick, clothing the naked, and feeding the hungry. In this same context, he also stated, "I was a stranger and you welcomed me" (Matt 25:35). Jesus focused especially on strangers, thus taking up Old Testament traditions: "When an alien resides with you in your land, you shall not oppress the alien" (Lev 19:33); "You shall not abhor any of the Edomites, for they are your kin. You shall not abhor any of the Egyptians, because you were an alien residing in their land" (Deut 23:7). The memory of their own fate and their life in exile was meant to make the Israelites open toward strangers among them. In practice, however, that is sure to have had its limits, since only membership in the tribe could guarantee the safety necessary for living one's life.

But Jesus radicalized the love for one's neighbor and for the alien and proclaimed the kingdom of God, where everyone is at home. As Paul writes, "So then you are no longer strangers and aliens, but you are citizens with the saints and also members of the household of God" (Eph 2:19). This radical membership in God's kingdom makes membership in ethnic or cultural groups highly relative. Everyone is a member of the same household.

St. Benedict (480–547) tried to realize the same ideal in his monasteries. At a time when migration was mixing up ethnic groupings, he offered a home for anyone. The "Benedictine Peace" (*pax benedictina*) envelops those born poor and rich, free and enslaved (see the *Rule of Benedict*, 2:16–20). We know from Benedict's biographer, Pope Gregory I, that Goths and other foreign tribes were represented in Benedict's monasteries as well.

It is remarkable how often Jesus held up "aliens" or strangers as role models: the famous good Samaritan (see Luke 10:25–37) is only one example. It is not a Jew who holds the moral high ground, but the foreigner. Of the ten lepers healed by Jesus, only one returned to express gratitude (see Luke 17:11–19), and he, too, was a Samaritan, not a member of the Chosen People of Israel. When Jesus encountered a Roman centurion who asked for one of his servants to be healed, Jesus was astonished: "Truly I tell you, in no one in Israel have I found such faith" (Matt 8:5-13). And this man was found among the Romans, among the hated occupiers.

Strangers in our own land, in our own hometown, and most of all strangers in our own house are a litmus test of our missionary spirit. Are we capable of transcending ourselves and seeing differences as an enrichment rather than a threat—not necessarily because of the beauties of multiculturalism but because all people are children of God? As missionary Benedictines, we have found it very challenging for many cultures to live under a single roof, and sometimes it doesn't work at all. This is not a "nice" process we are talking about, but receiving the stranger as Christ involves serious work and effort.

Being a missionary and being a stranger are inextricably linked. On the one hand, anyone who wants to be a missionary, who wants to bear witness, also needs to have a certain joy in encountering and being a stranger. Otherness must interest and attract him. On the other hand, the missionary is automatically an alien when he sets out: he goes into a foreign country or foreign culture and encounters others on their home soil, not his. He depends on acceptance by locals and must humbly search for the appropriate way of talking about the gospel.

By holding the stranger up as an ideal, Jesus is also blessing all missionaries and all those who dare to venture into foreign cultures—because there, these people are themselves strangers. Being a stranger can contain a special kind of blessing, if one encounters others with a respectful and loving heart.

## Cultures learn from one another

Whether one lives in a country of immigrants or not, people of diverse cultures often live close together. The Christian faith can offer a framework for how cultures can peacefully learn and profit from one another. Let's consider some examples. Not all come from our immediate surroundings, but looking at different countries and the world mission is especially useful for gaining new perspectives on what is happening closer to home. When I talk about "missionaries," therefore, I am not drawing attention to exotic lands and men and women in white robes, but instead encouraging you to apply these stories to our local situations. That is a defining characteristic of missionary work in a globalized world.

As early as the 1980s, the missionary Benedictine Congregation of St. Ottilien began to base their work on the motto "Intercultural Learning." Gradually, they had realized that mission cannot be a one-way street, but that the missionary must also have a listening heart: the missionary receives as much as he gives of himself, and he can give of himself only as much as he listens. Getting to know the other culture enriches one's own culture and spiritual life. After decades of trying to impose a European style of Benedictine practice in Africa, this realization helped give rise to a genuine African Benedictine tradition.

The old model of missionary work wasn't always aware of its own cultural implications. It brought not only a religion, but also a culture, and the danger was not only that one erased valuable aspects of the local culture, but that the local people were more interested in the new way of life than in the faith itself. What was foreign was attractive and seemed to hold benefits. In encounters with foreign ways of life, the missionary therefore needs to be a learner as well. A fellow brother who had spent a great deal of time as a pastor among Native Americans in Indian reservations once told that he had just offered Mass in a small village in North Dakota and had planned on leaving just after lunch. But the Native Americans said to him, "Father, sit down and stay with us. You're like a mosquito, you come, eat, and take off." Not a very flattering comment, but one that made my fellow brother think. How hectic our own culture is! To him, it was an invitation to try and go slower.

The pastor of my hometown in Germany, who was born in the Congo, once told me a different story:

> One moment, which was among the most difficult of my practice, occurred during a visit to a very ill woman. At the very beginning of our conversation in her home, the woman—who had called for the priest herself—said to me: "I actually didn't want to talk to a Catholic priest. I'm sorry, pastor, but white Catholic priests are stupid, they know nothing about life. You're a Catholic priest as well, but you come from a different cultural world." After this hardly friendly introduction, the woman explained her situation. She had pancreatic cancer, and her doctor's prognosis gave her only four weeks to live. Her stories let me feel how deeply the woman was suffering from the thought that she might be punished by God, and from her past with the Church. So many things in her life seemed to have remained unresolved. So, I began by thanking her for her trust. Then I tried to explain that I could not promise to have the right answer for her and her situation and her questions. At the end of our conversation, the woman was relieved and grateful for my visit. My words, she told me, had given her courage and strength for the coming days.[8]

This encounter is another wonderful example of how the otherness of a culture can open new doors. The woman was able to trust the priest precisely because he was black.

Encountering other cultures requires a special sensitivity. Companies who send their young employees to other continents to establish branch offices expect that these employees demonstrate "intercultural skills." Those include flexibility, clear communication, and empathy; but the ability to put ourselves in someone else's shoes, a willingness to learn, the ability to deal well with criticism, acquiring and understanding new information quickly, interest in learning a foreign language, and a consciousness of our own cultural background can also help us forge connections with others over religious topics.

In terms of the targeted acquisition of knowledge, I find Wikipedia an excellent tool for intercultural learning. For example, I will look up a term first in German and then in English. It's unbelievable what differences in a definition can be found on one and the same subject, or even just in the length of the articles! For example, on the topic of "advertising," German Wikipedia has many pages, most of them talking about the dangers of advertising. The English page is much shorter; in the United States, advertising is a fact of everyday life and is not seen as problematic. The more languages you speak, the faster you can find such cultural differences—and discovering other cultures is fun!

Encountering and even living with other cultures is never completely free of conflict. But learning happens precisely through those conflicts. If one can meet cultural differences with good humor, the first step has already been made. As the missionary and Verbum Dei sister Julia Prinz says, "Missionaries build bridges between cultures." She gives an example from the experience of her own congregation: The Verbum Dei sisters who live in the order's San Francisco house come from a variety of different countries and continents. In the house, they all live, pray, work, and eat together: "A Spaniard, a German, a Mexican, and a Singaporean Chinese are all sitting together at table and need something from the neighboring table. The Spaniard will stand up and take what she needs without saying a word. The German will stand up and ask, 'Do you need the salt?' in a friendly voice, and after hearing 'no,' takes it. The Mexican stands up and asks, 'Do you need the pepper?' and expects that to be understood as asking for the pepper. After a while, she simply takes it and sits down. The Singaporean Chinese gets up and stands at the table looking at the ketchup, nonverbally signaling her desire for it. But unless she is asked, she will neither take it nor sit down. Each of the sisters thinks that their own behavior is normal, while others may find it arrogant, difficult, or frustrating—depending on the cultural background."[9]

And, finally, there is an example that I was fortunate to experience and that highlights cultural differences within Germany. I was looking for a place in former East Germany to establish a monastery. We finally discovered a lovely small town on an island in the Baltic Sea. Just like everywhere else in the area, probably 90 percent of the villagers were not baptized. Many of them, too, certainly felt some connection to the communism they had lived under. By coincidence, I arrived the very day of a village celebration. I was traveling in my monk's habit and wondered for a moment whether I should take it off. I was afraid that in this environment I would look like I had come from a different planet. But in prayer, I heard the reassurance to keep wearing the clothes of my order.

In the square where the celebrations were taking place, I met a family with whom I was good friends, and we talked animatedly at a side table. Repeatedly, I felt others looking darts at me that I read as: Who is that strange man here in his black robe, what does he want here? Because one of the people with whom I was talking was a young woman, a large, bearded islander felt compelled to check whether everything was alright. He walked toward me and asked who I was. I introduced myself. "Well, you never know," he said, a little apologetically. He was right, because these days you can't always trust priests, either. And so, a pleasant conversation developed. In the end, he asked me to come to the other table, where most of the islanders were sitting. All were very friendly and offered me sausages. After the sausages came the beer. And after the beer, a digestive brandy. And another one, and so forth and so on. All the while, we had a lively exchange of stories about everything and anything, or literally, as we say in German, about God and the world. It was one of my most joyful missionary experiences. Nothing came of the attempt to establish the monastery, but I will never forget this encounter. Completely alien cultures collided here: Catholic and atheist, Bavarian (by choice) and islander (by birth), monk and fisherman. We attracted one another precisely because we were so different—at least, after the initial fear had been conquered.

## Criticizing cultures

The Christian faith wants to inculturate itself. God made all people and loves their respective life contexts. But these contexts may not always be good: every culture has its weak points, points that keep us from fulfilling our humanity. Here, too, faith has something to give; it can offer constructive criticism to the cultures.

The Second Vatican Council, known as Vatican II, completed the great paradigm shift by which mission means inculturation.[10] Based on negative experiences of missionary imperialism, the Church has become humble and has instructed its missionaries to preach the gospel, not your own culture! Do not force the other to accept your culture under the guise of accepting Christ. Because Christ always respected and accepted others in their individuality.

In an interesting development, this change in the under-standing of missionary work now means that missionaries are often better informed about local cultures than many locals themselves. There are countless examples of the paradox that one doesn't always know best the things one is closest to. It always impresses me how Fr. Severin, who has been one of our missionaries in Tanzania for decades now, reminds the local population of their own culture and helps uncover its meanings. He can do so because he has studied the local culture inten-sively, beginning with the local language. By asking and study-ing, he helps preserve the cultures he finds. This kind of mission is far removed from the charge of imperialism. Instead, it is the very opposite; it tries to help people find themselves.

By now, a new development is apparent. Western cultures, especially, have become largely secular. Religion has evapo-rated. The problem for the new evangelization is that here, inculturation will not get us far. *Into what* can we inculturate Christianity when there is no more culture, or only a very shal-low one, or even a kind of anti-culture, harming people more than it helps them? Should we adapt to a "culture" of fast food when what we are talking about is the Eucharist, the Last Supper? Instead, can't a culture of the meal as a celebration help to invest our joint meals with more meaning and form? Should we adapt ourselves to a society that has given up almost all taboos? Should we not instead pass on an unassailable respect for God so that our respect for human dignity can remain just as unassailable and protected?

When parts of the Church advocate a retreat from the worldly, as Pope Benedict XVI discussed in his Freiburg lecture, this should not lead churches to avoid making statements and staying in some "holy niche." Instead, we should take Jesus' words that we are from below and he is from above, that he is not of the same world as we are (see John 8:23; 17:16), as encouragement to preserve an inner distance from our own culture, to help make it more humane. In this sense, the Christian culture can be a provocative counterculture.

The Christian faith has the potential to be critical of culture—it feeds itself in transcendence and can therefore transcend any culture. That is something I see in my current hometown of Schuyler, Nebraska, in the American Midwest. In this small town, Catholic immigrants from Mexico and Catholic Anglo-Americans of originally German or Czech descent flow together into a single congregation. Now, which is more Catholic, North American Catholicism or Hispanic Catholicism? There are significant differences in mentality, but also significant differences in piety. While many Anglo-Americans dutifully donate a great deal of money to their congregations, many Hispanics send all they have left over to their relatives back in Central and South America. But they also use amenities that the congregation provides. One can see both sides, and conflicts are of course unavoidable. But while church attendance among Anglo-Americans is decreasing (even though it's still at a very high rate compared with Germany), the Hispanic minority can often be seen praying, and very expressively, too. They sometimes spend hours of their time kneeling before the altar. Who is "right" and who is "better"?

Christian culture can help us transcend our own culture—it's just sad that it doesn't succeed everywhere. In some countries, particularly in some parts of Africa, different tribes go to war although they are connected by faith. But Christ is one and the same, on one side as much as the other. "There is no longer Jew or Greek, there is no longer slave or free, there is no longer male and female; for all of you are one in Christ Jesus" (Gal 3:28). The Church has always had the equanimity of spirit to not force a confrontation between diverse cultural backgrounds. Everywhere in the world, congregations come together based on their members' respective mother tongues: Italian congregations in Stuttgart, Polish ones in Hanover, and so on. Nevertheless, the missionary dimension of the Church also requires us not to isolate ourselves from one another but to at least stay in communication and contact.

Any culture, if it really is a culture, has advantages and disadvantages, good sides and problematic sides. Paul the missionary counsels, "Test everything; hold fast to what is good" (1 Thess 5:21), and Pope Gregory the Great recommends, "Observe everything, pass over much, correct little."[11] The Christian faith can help us to "cleanse" cultures, to bring out their positive aspects and critically question the negative ones.

In his missionary journeys, Paul found that the cross, as the central sign of the redemption of Christians, cannot be co-opted by cultures: "We proclaim Christ crucified, a stumbling block to Jews and foolishness to Gentiles" (1 Cor 1:23). The cross, in the truest sense of the word, crosses the traditions and rites that people have practiced in order to attain happiness. In that way, the center of Christianity already contains a counterculture. In this respect, St. Benedict is very clear in his rule. Since there are people of the most varied ethnic and cultural backgrounds under the roof of his monastery—such as former slaves and freeborns, or Italians and Goths, who outside of the cloister were not "on speaking terms"—he admonishes the abbot: "The only grounds on which in Christ's eyes one is to be preferred to another is by excelling in good works and humility. The abbot or abbess, then, should show equal love to all and apply the same standards of discipline to all, according to what they deserve."[12]

Dr. Ansgar Stüfe, OSB, a long-time missionary to Tanzania, describes how one can bring a greater humanity to found cultures:

In every culture, there are different ways of dealing with suffering. In Africa, experiences of suffering are often explained magically: ancestors have been angered by the incorrect behavior of individuals, and through their anger, the ancestors have caused the individual to suffer. Such an explanation, or a variation of it, occurs in almost all countries in sub-Saharan Africa. One of the couples with us, both doctors, lost their second child at the age of four months for unknown reasons, probably a congenital heart defect. But a single woman had visited the doctors the day before, and now the locals said that she had caused the death of the child out of spite. The husband reacted by inviting all employees, friends, and acquaintances over to hold a memorial service at the couple's home six weeks after the child's death. The rector of the local seminary—a family friend—held mass. Vast numbers of people came. There were some I had never seen in a single service anywhere in the area. After the gospel reading, the doctor stood up and made a personal plea. He said that his family had suffered much but that no one was to blame. As Christians, he said, they all believed in resurrection, and that their children were now representing their family in heaven.

One could have heard a pin drop during that speech. For me, this was the deepest missionary experience I have ever had, and it changed my faith. A real-life situation was overcome by faith and simultaneously became a testament for others. Our doctor's aim, of course, had nothing whatsoever to do with bearing emotionally powerful witness; he was simply trying to free himself from magical thinking. His wife had far greater problems doing so, but she too eventually succeeded in freeing herself.[13]

Br. Ansgar gives yet another example in which faith questions culture:

One day, a woman was admitted to the hospital with skin abrasions, hematomas, and breathing problems. Her husband had beaten her. I ordered an X-ray of her lungs and saw spots on both sides of the lung. One day later, the woman died of lung failure, and since it had been caused by violence, we had to perform an autopsy. We discovered that the lung tissue was damaged all over, with non-localized bleeding. This bleeding caused the lung failure. I later learned that the husband had stepped on his wife as she lay on the floor, and that this had caused the internal injuries.

This occurrence gave me great disgust for the African culture, because violence against women happens daily there, even if not always as grievously as in this case. At the time, I wondered whether this culture might not be completely pathological. It took me some time to achieve a little more distance from it, though violence toward women and children fills me with loathing to this day. But my hatred has become more relative through the abuse scandals in our own country; all cultures have their dark sides. I still, however, do not have an answer to such shocking occurrences. I believe that evil can be kept at bay, at least, only through the counterweight of lived faith. I have given up the illusion that evil can be conquered. But it can be kept at bay.

As someone from the outside, it is hard to criticize a culture. We might be reproached: "What do you know about it, you're not one of us." One may see the good and the bad more clearly, but in the end, cultures must change from within. In that context, our task as missionaries is to question the things we experience, and to provide an alternative. We can do nothing more. But that is already a great deal. And it requires that we present ourselves as we are, and with all we believe.

## Homelessness

"The missionary spirit lives from remaining foreign," says Julia Prinz. Anyone who encounters foreign countries or foreign cultures in one's own country steps outside the familiar and is no longer at home.

Jesus knows all about this feeling: "Foxes have holes, and birds of the air have nests; but the Son of Man has nowhere to lay his head" (Luke 9:58). And we do see Jesus wander from village to village, from region to region during the time of his preaching and healing. That is a role model for missionaries and any people who dare to proclaim their convictions while encountering others. If I go outside myself, then I must also leave my home. That may be on a large scale—my country, my culture, my mother tongue. Or it can be on a small scale—my habits, my security, my traditions. As a missionary, I'm exposed in much the same way as Jesus chose to be exposed to strangers and those on the margins of society.

Often, that isn't easy at all, and can even involve suffering. I went off to my mission in the United States with my banners held aloft with pride, so to speak. But I hadn't imagined how strong my longing for "home" would be. I experienced what is known in intercultural communication as "culture shock." The things that make one feel alienated are, first and foremost, ridiculously trivial. For example: While standing at the checkout at Walmart, I'm rummaging through my wallet and can't readily identify the coins that I need to pay. A doctor asks me my height and weight, and I can't give him an immediate answer (at least not in feet, inches, and pounds). When I was in Ireland on a language course, I properly stopped at a pedestrian traffic light, until little children called to me, "You aren't from here?" Very probably, none of the locals bothered with the traffic laws at that crossing. Though I looked European, I was still immediately obvious as a stranger. How difficult must it be to look foreign as well! Our African missionaries keep telling me that as a white European, you simply can't hide in a crowd of Africans. The white face immediately stands out in between the black. Just imagine how it must be in reverse for people in our latitudes who are visibly different from most of our compatriots by either their looks or their behavior. Even if, after a time, one gets used to the new country and the new people, there is always a certain homelessness. One is always slightly apart. I find that to be particularly interesting in our old missionaries who return home after fifty or more years in Africa. Their former home has changed so much that they no longer feel at home—but they're strangers in the land of their mission, too. They seem to have no home any more in any of their countries.

The Irish monks of the fifth and sixth centuries called this a "white martyrdom," in contrast with the red martyrdom, because your blood is not necessarily spilled when you become a missionary. That may sound drastic, but there is some truth to it. A missionary makes the sacrifice of giving up a home, and that sacrifice is painful. But it can also give you wings. The productivity, joy, and fruitfulness of missionaries are grounded in precisely this sacrifice. Because they were not born where they now live, they are especially dependent on making contacts, on getting to know the land, the people, the language. They develop a specific energy. Often, missionaries get to know their "mission territory" better than locals.

But this homelessness inspires them not only to explore and adopt many of the traditions and friendships with people around them, it also inspires them to sink their roots more deeply into God. "But our citizenship is in heaven," says Paul the Apostle in his Epistle to the Philippians (3:20). Just like Jesus himself, missionaries have no other home, and they recognize this particularly when they are on their own. They have left their homeland not because it is so terrible, but because they have been sent by one who has become their deeper home. When we bear witness to faith, we should purposely expose ourselves to this lack of a home. We should set out with no bag and no sandals, trusting that we will find someone who will nourish us: "Remain in the same house, eating and drinking whatever they provide, for the laborer deserves to be paid" (Luke 10:7).

If we encounter strangers from a place of homelessness, then we are both foreign, both strangers. That opens doors to getting to know and trust one another.

## A MONK'S PERSPECTIVE

### The "monk" and "missionary"

Monks are people who leave everything behind, live cut off in their monasteries, and have thus bid their farewell to the world. This *fuga mundi* or "flight from the world" is an old trait of monasticism. St. Benedict was disgusted by the city of Rome and the mores he found there, so much that he broke off his studies and went off to live in solitude. The first monks in Egypt retreated into the desert, far away from civilization. They lived in caves and mountains and sought God undisturbed, as hermits.

What is astonishing is that it is precisely in the monasteries that crucial developments for Church and society originated. Why is that and what can monks contribute to mission and to evangelization—what impulses can we deduce for our lives today?

The missionary Benedictines of St. Ottilien were founded in the nineteenth century by the Benedictine monk Andreas Amrhein (1844-1927), who envisioned a closer connection between monasticism and mission. That idea was not new but had been a widespread practice since late antiquity. First, Amrhein sent monks to the then German parts of East Africa, and then to Korea. More than 130 years later, the missionary Benedictines have helped create blossoming local churches across four continents, and most of the development projects in the regions where our monasteries lie have been initiated and shepherded by Benedictine monks. It began with the purchase of slaves in order to then grant them their freedom, and soon extended to founding childcare facilities, orphanages, schools, and hospitals and medical centers, all of which are still highly significant today. Monks were just as dedicated to improving access to fresh water for the locals as they were to the development of more efficient agriculture. Over the years, they also managed to get locals interested and, in some cases, enthusiastic about monastic life. Today, our monasteries in Tanzania, Kenya, Zambia, Uganda, South Africa, Togo, Venezuela, Colombia, Cuba, South Korea, China, and India are almost entirely self-sufficient.

Then something unexpected happened. While we had been focusing all that energy on "the missions" (meaning third world countries) in the first century, the need in our home countries came to be felt more and more strongly. There was growing demand for the schools we run in Europe—and they were no longer merely "mission seminaries" for training monks, but a popular alternative to state schools for people of all faiths. The demand for our guest and retreat houses grew, as well. Countless people make use of them to escape the stress of their everyday life, to gain some perspective in silence, in prayer, and in conversation with the monks.

What makes a monastery so appealing? It's difficult to find an answer to that question, particularly as a monk. In many ways, monks live something very different from most of society. I don't mean just that they wear the habit of their order, but rather, for example, individual monks do not have an income and the monastery serves as a community with shared property. Then there are minor things, such as the fact that we leave our work whenever the bell rings and go to prayer; that we get up at 4:30 a.m. to have time for praying and reading the Bible; that we are silent during meals, and instead read to one another from a book; or that we intone chants that are over a thousand years old and recite prayers that were prayed three thousand years ago. To anyone who lives this life, it is completely normal, but for outsiders, it is alien, and often fascinating at first. What is alien can be attractive, as well. The French philosopher Michel Foucault coined the term "heterotopia" ("else-where" or "other-place") to describe the experience that there are some places where everything is suddenly completely different. As examples, he cites prisons, hospitals, and graveyards, for when we go there, our old routines no longer apply. Insignificant things become important, while things we cannot do without suddenly lose their significance. In certain ways, a monastery is just such a "heterotopia."

If we see monasteries in this light, then suddenly the missionary perspective is inverted: monks don't go out into the world, people come to them. Monks don't go to foreign countries, they are the foreigners who are visited. In his rule, the founder of our order admonishes us that monks should remain strangers to the workings of the world: *Saeculi actibus se facere alienum* (Rule of St. Benedict 4:20).

In fact, it is the case that when a monastery starts to adapt to its surroundings too much, it loses not only its charm but also its justification and successive generations of monks. This happens when it takes up unthinkingly those things that are common in the mainstream, when it "compromises" and loses the focus on finding God. But if a monk lives convincingly, he has a practical missionary radiance, and the liturgy, for example, becomes a way of quietly bearing witness. There is an old saying: "The monks' pulpit is choral prayer." Seeing grown men or women pray together is moving, and that is precisely what monks do, regardless of whether there is a visitor in the church or not. They radiate the unconditionality of their way of life. So being a monk does not exclude being a missionary. Instead, "monk" and "missionary" are mutually enriching. Only when a monk has truly become a stranger to this world can he help others (from his own cultural circle!) distance themselves from their lives and gain new access to God. By "leaving the world," he transcends his life and opens himself up to the divine. It is from there that anything new enters the world.

Conversely, the attributes of a "monk" can be useful for a "missionary." One of the central characteristics of monastic life is asceticism, and following Jesus' advice, the missionary, too, should "travel light." A missionary must live a simple life of few demands. As the missionary Paul says, "Athletes exercise self-control in all things; they do it to receive a perishable wreath, but we an imperishable one" (1 Cor 9:25).

The ninth-century Benedictine monk St. Ansgar, himself a missionary, coined the classic formula *intimus monachus, foris apostolus* ("inwardly a monk, outwardly one who has been sent"). Today, we might expand this formula by saying, "Inwardly a missionary, outwardly a monk," or more explicitly: constantly convert yourself, and when you show your faith outwardly, do so as humbly as a monk.

This approach can help us if we want to find ways of showing our faith more clearly in our everyday life and surroundings. We may feel ourselves protected and cared for, as if surrounded by cloister walls or robed in a habit. In other words, whatever I show here and however it may be received, it is important to me—this is how I act, this is how I believe. Furthermore, monasteries can encourage us to be different, to show ourselves. We monks did not think, "We want to be different so that people will come to us." We just do what we believe, regardless of what others think. Why *not* pray before a meal? Why should we be embarrassed in front of our guests if we think it right and good? After all, we aren't forcing them to make it their tradition.

For all the "isolation" of monastic life, there is another element that marks out a monk's life, and that element is hospitality. In his rule, St. Benedict writes that a monk should be convinced that in his guest he is welcoming Christ himself.[14] Monks try to live this respect, awe, and openness. When entering the monastery, no one is asked, Are you Catholic? No one's way of life is questioned or even examined. Everyone is welcome, as this is a house of God. And God joyfully takes in everyone, especially the poor and strangers. The culture of hospitality is something wonderful that anyone can cultivate in their own context. Instead of cutting myself off from the world, I am signaling to others that they are worth my time, that they are worth my effort.

In other words, the missionary paradigm has changed. We are now very far from the "conquering" and "recruiting" approach and are opening ourselves to a culture of missionary work that is open and hospitable to all who want to learn something about faith.

But "monk" and "missionary" have been highly complementary roles in the past, as well, as examples from history show. Bede the Venerable, a monk and church historian from the seventh and eighth century, described the monks as "ideal" missionaries due to the "simplicity of their innocent life and the sweetness of their divine teaching."[15] St. Gregory the Great, who was a monk before being elected Pope (540–604), is another good example. He himself preferred the contemplative life and saw outside contacts as a burden, but he nevertheless sent Augustine of Canterbury and other monks to England in 595, thus setting off a movement that brought Christianity into Europe's northernmost corners. Because of this missionary significance, Gregory is seen as "heir to Paul," writing a biography of Benedict and supporting the missionaries to England with his letters.[16] The British (then still Anglo-Saxon) Isles in turn gave rise to a very important missionary-monastic impulse for Germanic countries.[17]

After the first mission to South Germany by the Irish monk Kilian (640–89) and his fellow monk Pirmin's (ca. 670–755) mission to southwestern Germany and Alsace, St. Boniface (ca. 673–755) arrived in Franconia in Southern Germany. A Benedictine monk himself, he did not leave England until he was forty years old. His missionary goal was to stabilize the Church through the local clergy and a Christian culture, which he tried to encourage by building monasteries, such as the ones he founded in Ohrdruf, Fritzlar, Amöneburg, and Fulda. This cultural countermovement in the Christian spirit advocated chastity (particularly for the clergy, but also in monogamous marriage), low regard for property (avoidance of avarice), obedience, no warlike behavior (avoidance of weapons, no killing, not even hunting), and education. Much of this he achieved, though there are many areas in which he didn't succeed, as his failure in Frisia demonstrates.

Today, we live in a completely different time, but the principle of "heterotopias" inspired by and modeling Christian values has remained the same. A Christian missionary who had studied Islamic teachings closely once told me that Islamic morality had somewhat "monastic" aspects. In certain ways, Islam (or an aspect of it) seeks to order people's ways of life with a strictness and consistency that in Christianity are lived only in monasteries. Consequently, the ideal of these teachings is that all of society will one day live as if in a monastery (regarding clothing, times of prayer, fasting, etc.). The entire world should become a monastery. Clearly, this is incompatible with the open societies of the West.

The Christian idea is different. Anyone who voluntarily wants to submit him or herself to the particularly strict Christian observance as a monk may do so and thus become a model for others. But Benedictines have never wanted to turn the entire world into a monastery. Instead, their way of life is a reaction to the words of Jesus: "You are the salt of the earth; but if salt has lost its taste, how can its saltiness be restored? It is no longer good for anything, but is thrown out and trampled under foot" (Matt 5:13). The Order of St. Benedict do not see themselves as the soup, but as this salt of the earth, and just a little salt is enough for giving the whole soup its flavor.[18] But this little bit of salt should not lose its taste. It is a concentrate. There are only about seven thousand male monks in the world, but their influence is strong, particularly when it comes to education, hospitality, and social causes. This form of mission is so modern because of the freedom it allows the people who are being missionized. They are invited and can come if and when they like.

They can leave again and return to their own world and freely decide what part of their newly learned Christian teaching they want to apply to their lives. This cuts off at the root any suspicions of a pseudo-imperialist takeover. The monks are open to all Christian denominations, to people of no faith who are searching, and to dialogue with people of other faiths. What they expect is not primarily entrance into the order or even conversion, but only respect for their way of life.

## Contemplation

Let's get more precise about how monks encounter the world. One good example for this tradition is given by the Benedictine Pope Gregory the Great in his biography of St. Benedict:[19] An extremely brutal Goth by the name of Zalla rampages and pillages, finally happening upon a poor farmer whose property he wants to seize. To gain time, the farmer tells a lie and claims to have given everything to Benedict, so that he may get away from the brutal man. At that, Zalla stops torturing the farmer and binds his arms. He tells him to go to this Benedict who has received all his wealth, and follows the poor farmer, arms bound, to Benedict's monastery, where the great man is sitting at the gate reading. When the farmer tells Zalla that this is Benedict, Zalla becomes angry and hopes to get his way with fury and intimidation. He screams at Benedict, "Stand up! Give me what you have received from this man!" Benedict calmly looks up from his reading and sees both Zalla and the bound farmer. But as soon as he looks at the farmer's bonds, they fall off faster than any human hand could untie them. The farmer who had arrived bound is now fully free. Fearful of such power, Zalla falls to the ground and bends his neck, throws himself at Benedict's feet and offers himself in prayer, forswearing his violent ways. But the holy man does not get up from his reading, and calls brothers to lead Zalla into the monastery, instead, and to offer him altar bread. When Zalla is brought back to him, he admonishes him to leave his cruelty, and Zalla goes off chastened, no longer daring to take anything from the farmer after a man of God had freed him by a mere look.

At first, this looks like just an uplifting piece of hagiography and the story of a miracle. But it contains a great deal of truth. Benedict, the monk, is engrossed in reading the Holy Scripture, and *lectio divina*—prayerful contemplation of holy texts—is indeed a fundamental and daily practice of monks. Instead of actively intervening in the chaos and injustice of the world, a monk lets "the world" come to him. He looks up from his Bible and sees the brutality and viciousness that are happening in front of him—but his eyes were resting on the blessed, healing words of Scripture. Through the power of the holy Word, he looks at the situation and solves it immediately. He does not even require touch—a monk does not let himself become entangled in the world; a look is enough. Benedict does not even get up. After his admonishment, he returns his gaze to God's book and simply keeps reading. Mission that comes from contemplation, or as the monastic tradition says, *contemplata tradere*—passing on the observed: That is the contribution of monks to healing the world. That is their mission. A contemplative look disentangles the knots of this world. The loving look from God's perspective can heal and save us.

When we watch the news every day, when we experience conflicts in our workplace or in our families that bring us to the edge of our capacity, how can we offer appropriate help? It's possible that intervening, even to defend someone, pulls us into the maelstrom ourselves. The monastic perspective, on the contrary, is this: Stay centered in yourself. Take care only of what is your part in the whole story. Communicate hope. Communicate the hope that God will help, and draw on God's power when you help and when you do intervene, so that you remain in contact with God whatever happens. Otherwise, you will be in touch with negative forces such as envy, hate, and revenge. Anyone who wants to draw on his faith for others is invited to remain in constant contact with God just like a monk—practicing prayer and meditation often, so that he is let go and has also let go in a way that helps others solve their problems.

Another story from Benedict's life clarifies this approach to the world. Shortly before his death, Benedict is standing at the window of his cell and sees the entire world in a sunbeam, as if in a revelation. Looking at the world outside, which is completely dark (it is night), he witnesses a light pouring down from above and illuminating everything around him. Seeing the entire world as if contained in a beam of sunlight is a miraculous experience for him, an enlightening moment, so to speak.[20] In the story, we can see how the missionary principle is turned inside out: the monk's heart becomes the macrocosm and the world the microcosm.[21] In his eyes, the world is very small, but his heart sees it as completely illuminated and loved by God. It is this world to which he bears witness.

The monk's relationship with the world is marked by two contrary directions: in one case by distance. We are invited to see the world as less important than it sees and often portrays itself. There is so much hysteria, so much excitement, and too quick, unconsidered, and unblessed reacting, which often make things much worse. We should not let ourselves be carried away but instead stay at home in our solitude.

The other direction comes to us in the study of Scripture, when "our heart becomes large." In this moment, we become truly capable of *compassion*, of empathy, of contributing honestly to the improvement of this world.

For example, a married couple who has been coming to talk with me for a long time has been babysitting their now adolescent grandchildren regularly for years. It suddenly becomes clear that one of these children has repeatedly touched the other inappropriately. But the mother of the perpetrator cannot accept this truth, and the family is breaking apart from the accusations and lawyer's visits. The grandparents, who are innocent, have closed their house to the adolescent perpetrator, and are suffering from the split in the large family. They wonder how they can unite the family again, but our conversation reveals that there is not much they can do. The responsibility lies with their daughter, whose son is the perpetrator and who herself is victimized by the narcissism and violence of her husband, whom she cannot bring herself to divorce. What the grandparents can do is to support their daughter, not give up their hope, and pray for all involved. They recognize that they can do good only by letting go. In this way, they increase the effectiveness of their contribution.

In the same way, Benedict's preferred place is "on the doorstep." He sits on the border between sanctity and the world. That should be our place as well. We should neither draw back completely from the world nor let ourselves be drawn completely into it. On this border, on this doorstep, we can draw on the Holy, and simultaneously do good works outward into the world.

4

# BEARING WITNESS

Thinking about the possible themes that emerge when we talk about faith and religion, it's natural to be worried about whether one will come up with the right words at the right time—especially if one isn't completely familiar with a topic or if one doesn't have a clearly formed opinion. For many years now, I have given courses—called "New Evangelization: Task and Joy," or, in German contexts, "When I am asked about my faith..."—containing an exercise that never fails to touch and amaze me. It is based on an interview style developed by the German television station ZDF: the reporters provide the beginning of a sentence, and a prominent politician must complete it on the spur of the moment. The goal, of course, is to get the politician to reveal his true thoughts and feelings.

In our context, every participant has time to think up half sentences that refer to religion, faith, the meaning of life, the Church, or similar topics, such as "I imagine life after death is a lot like..."; "If I were the pope, I'd..."; "For me, confession means..."; "My favorite prayer is..."; and so on. Then we place two chairs in the center of the room and I ask two volunteers to sit on them. The first reads out her or his sentences, and the second must answer immediately, without thinking. Then they switch.

And here is where everyone is surprised by the experience. Even though there's always some initial nervousness (in a very real sense, you're in "the hot seat," and highly personal experiences are being discussed in a public setting), there has never been a person who was unable to give good, friendly, rational, enlightening answers spontaneously. This amazes everyone, me included. No subject is too intimate, nothing too theological or political for the volunteers to come up with a satisfying answer. Many participants had never even thought about some of the topics before, but they were still able to answer. I have only one explanation for this experience, and that is Jesus' promise that we should "not worry about how you are to speak or what you are to say; for what you are to say will be given to you at that time" (Matt 10:19).

Of course, in these retreats, there is always an atmosphere of mutual respect and interest, which may not be the case at work, on the street, in our neighborhood, or wherever we may be called upon to speak about these topics with others. But we may still trust that the Holy Spirit will act in us at that time if we go into our encounters with the knowledge that God trusts us to say something and the other person is worth our good and honest answer. In fact, Jesus gave this promise in the context of persecution. Christians who are accused and stand trial should not have any worries about their defense. Certainly, or at least hopefully, most of us are spared this situation, and the little moments in which we are called to give witness are nowhere near as dramatic or dangerous. But there is still a special kind of anxiousness, and Jesus wants to lift that off us. But one of the insights of this exercise is that being questioned about faith can enrich our own faith. "Do your really believe in a life after death?" I need to take a stand in relation to this question. Maybe I have never really confronted it or have never been too clear on it myself. By not avoiding an answer but responding to the question, what *I* believe is revealed. It is a shame that we are so rarely asked about our faith. That is why, in this exercise, we can proactively ask others about theirs. It is a gift to them if we do so in a respectful and friendly way. It is a gift for both the questioner and the questioned, as the participants of the course experience over and over.

This exercise reveals, almost as if in a laboratory, what bearing witness is about. The answers must fulfill two conditions. First, they must be authentic. Just reciting the catechism is pointless. At the very least, a person might state, "I have experienced this myself, as well, and it has become very important to me personally," or, "This is actually difficult for me." Second, the answer must resonate with the person asking the question. A person will understand an answer when they can relate to what is being said. This doesn't mean giving only the answers that the other wants to hear, it may even be exactly the opposite. Instead, it is about feeling deeper and listening to what the other person is truly asking.

As an example, an old woman once told me that God certainly must be a merciful judge. What I *hear* is that she is a little fearful. She wants to be in harmony with God when she leaves this world, and, all in all, she does feel a part of this harmony. I could answer her by saying, "Yes, God is merciful. But he is also a judge." That would be correct as far as Christian teaching goes, but would it really help her? Instead, I respond in such a way that the woman can take courage from it, because that is what she really wants, and to have her contact with God strengthened. "Oh yes, God is merciful and kind. He sees all the good you have done, and he wants to forgive us for our sins."

Words are not all that is important for bearing witness. Tone, friendliness, and an atmosphere of respect are just as important. When we talk about faith, one of our greatest temptations is to justify ourselves. Our own experiences of faith are very personal, we want to know that they are taken seriously and accepted. But if they aren't, we quickly become defensive, aggressive, impatient, and stop perceiving the other. Jesus invites us to be fully serene. The Holy Spirit will take care of us. There's no need for us to defend or justify ourselves!

Luke describes the way in which the first Christians shared their faith as "boldness" (*parrhesia* in Greek), an inner freedom and serenity that could be felt in their words, a kind of mastery that could not come from the apostles themselves: "Now when they saw the boldness of Peter and John and realized that they were uneducated and ordinary men, they were amazed and recognized them as companions of Jesus" (Acts 4:13). We are invited to let ourselves go, to give ourselves completely to the Holy Spirit in situations of bearing witness. The Holy Spirit will allow us to choose not only the right words, but also the right way of saying them.

## OUR STORIES

Apart from spontaneous displays of our faith, we each carry a treasure within that we can draw on at any time of need: our stories. Each one of us, no matter how old, has had experiences in which he has been allowed to witness traces of the divine, in which she has met God or Christ. In evangelical churches, this is important for your story of "conversion" or your "turning point." Certainly, there are some exaggerations there, and no one should feel pressure or a need to compete over the impressiveness of their narratives. Instead, our stories should emerge naturally. It cannot be about boasting or bragging about my relationship with, experience of, or closeness to God. And we also need to avoid any kind of religious exhibitionism, where we talk too much and too intimately about ourselves and God. Just like any other relationship of love, our relationship with God requires that we have some secrets that are no one else's business.

In general, we don't talk enough about the stories of our life and faith. The stories in which God enters our lives are always exciting and inspiring. If we tell them humbly and remain in close contact with God and ourselves during the process, others can gather hope from them. The advantage of a story is that the listener can identify with it in whatever way he or she wants. The listener is free. In contrast, if I lay out a few propositions, the natural impulse is to dispute them. Stories leave all the freedom that is the fundamental precondition for good missionary work. Stories don't judge, and they protect the teller as well, because what is there to deny if that is how I have experienced this story? My brother once told me that he was hiking in the mountains on a very hot day and his water bottle was empty. He was already starting to panic when, directly in front of him, he discovered a stream he could drink from. Immediately, he remembered a psalm verse: "He will drink from the stream by the path; / therefore he will lift up his head" (Ps 110:7). My brother told this story so grippingly that to this day, when I pray on that psalm, I think of him. And each time, it inspires me again to trust more deeply in God. Our stories can only enrich us spiritually. And they don't even need to involve some extraordinary appearance of God or a conversion or something monumental. The incidental stories can be just as uplifting: a surprising instant of alignment during the day; being touched by nature; an encounter that makes me grateful and happy; a moment of comfort at a funeral; or a feeling of trust when standing before a statue of the Virgin Mary.

What spoke to my religious feelings? Which Bible passage is important to me or became real in my personal life? How has faith changed my day? What is my story with God? What connects me with the Church? Why did I become a Christian? Why am I still one? If any of these questions spark stories in you, tell them!

Telling stories puts us squarely in the Christian tradition because the Bible is full of them. It tells the story of what people have experienced with their God: how they were enslaved and he liberated them; how they hungered and he fed them even though that was hardly to be expected in the desert. The Gospels tell stories. We hear about Jesus and what he experienced with God and with people. And each of the evangelists tells the story in a slightly unique way—in *his* way, for his audience, but always about one and the same Christ. The lives of God and humanity are so interwoven that our only hope of reflecting them is in a narrative, that is, in a continuously told story. Such stories are infectious. If I hear someone else's story, I am encouraged to tell mine, as well. No two stories are the same, but because my story belongs to me, it is authentic and interesting. It doesn't need to be spectacular; the fact that God has entered my life is spectacular enough. How he chooses to do so is his business. Stories are probably one of the best ways of passing on faith in moral questions as well, and those questions are among the most difficult of all in religion. In moral theology, we talk about "narrative ethics": tell us about the experiences you had when you let yourself be guided by Christian morality in your job, in your marriage, in transitions. That's a better approach than simply postulating moral norms, even if they are clear and incontrovertible to you.

## OUR LANGUAGE

To understand someone else, I need to be able to understand their language. That is true of different languages like German, English, Swahili, and so on, just as much as it is of different language codes within one and the same language.

What made St. Paul such an effective missionary was that in addition to his mother tongue of Greek, he also spoke Latin (the main language of commerce at the time), Hebrew (the language of the theologians), and probably even Aramaic (Jesus' mother tongue and that of his disciples).[1] Language is a cultural carrier. It encodes cultural history, as anyone who has ever learned a foreign language will know. It's not just a question of learning grammar and vocabulary, but of getting to know other countries and other traditions as well. And it works in reverse—by getting to know another culture, you learn some of its language.

From a Christian point of view, all languages are expressions of the Holy Spirit. They are there to be understood. The Holy Spirit, in turn, is the understanding between the Father and the Son. God the Father sent his Son into the world as the first mission: Jesus was to spread the gospel *in His Spirit*. The Spirit becomes visible and audible in that moment in which someone is sent; it is what is between the Father and the Son, it is the way they understand one another. As such, the Holy Spirit is at the source of mission—no spirit, no mission. Pentecost, the Feast of the Holy Spirit, is the moment in which church and mission were born. Before that moment, the disciples had piously but fearfully locked themselves in their rooms. They did not know yet that they were sent, and they did not have the means for that mission: the power of the Holy Spirit. But then the miracle occurred, and they, the simple, and in some cases uneducated men and women, started to speak in all the tongues of the world. They spoke exactly those languages that the people outside their house spoke. This new communication had something intoxicating, and there were virtually no earthly explanations for how they had come to be able to communicate like this: "But others sneered and said, 'They are filled with new wine'" (Acts 2:13).

Early on in my missionary work in the United States, I recall sitting in the confessional of a church and a young man came in. He was of Mexican descent, and his English had a strong Hispanic accent. On top of that, he was speaking the language of youth, with its very own words and phrases. I answered him in my German-accented English as well as I could. In the background, there was meditative music playing, which the priest of the church had put on—a record of Gregorian chants, sung by monks from Heiligenkreuz. I knew this because I recognized the slightly Austrian accent to the Latin. In that moment, I was filled by a deep feeling of peace and joy. There I was, a German sitting in the middle of Nebraska, surrounded by English, Spanish, Austrian, and Latin, and the two of us—the youth and I—understood one another, connected by the Holy Spirit, connected by the forgiving and loving presence of God.

The Second Vatican Council introduced the mother tongue into the liturgy. This makes it maybe one of the most missionary of all the Catholic Church's councils. All Christians, it says, should be able to understand and pass on the gospel in their language. Liturgies had to be rewritten in each of the people's native tongues. It was an invitation to all of us to express the mystery of our faith in our own language and learn the languages of others; communicate so that we can spread the gospel.

Language expresses culture and way of life. Even in one and the same language, such as my native German, there are many different language codes. There are borders that run along regional lines, educational standards, migrant groups, and social settings. Several years ago, the churches discovered these different milieus for themselves. In terms of social access to certain groups in our society, the churches suddenly realized with alarm that they were unable to reach many different social settings. They simply weren't represented there any more, they didn't speak the language. Often, one was content to muse theoretically about the question, instead of heading out into these "unfamiliar" settings and learning how people there talk and think.

The language of our personal witnessing should open doors to God for others, not close them. Theological terms, for example, may be appropriate in theological discourse, but not in conversation with someone who doesn't understand them. Incidentally, it's a very good exercise for "professionals" to translate such terms into simpler language. Furthermore, within the church there is a kind of "slang," which helps people in the church realm feel at home. There isn't anything wrong with that, but once we recognize that we can no longer communicate outside that setting—at least regarding questions of faith—we should turn more to the people to better understand how they talk and think.

Learning someone else's language is an act of letting go. I must be able to *want* to tell something to the person across from me if I'm going to reach him with my words. Constantly, I find it both fascinating and terrifying when I notice that a press secretary or publicity representative is tasked with *not saying anything* at a specific moment. That sort of language is not helpful in bearing witness to God.

## HAVING COURAGE

> *I'm so liberal, I don't have a point of view. That's way too small-minded for me. You gotta be flexible, as well. And even when somebody asks me something, I just run away. I don't give him an answer. I don't wanna influence him! That's how liberal I am! You gotta wear that on your sleeve, gotta be in favor of everything.*
>
> —Sebastian Pufpaff, comedian

What Sebastian Pufpaff caricatures so wonderfully here is today's political correctness: complete openness to all sides, total liberalness. Anything rather than have a point of view. In this climate, we've learned to keep our opinions to ourselves unless we can be certain that they belong to the correct mainstream. We hold back because we don't want to disadvantage anyone. That's particularly true of religious questions. We don't even want to influence our own children. We mean for them to make up their own minds—but they do that anyway.

Just after I had become ordained a priest, I must have had this light in my eyes that probably shines in most newlyweds, as well. I was so full of love for God that I simply had to express my joy. A young family with whom I had struck up a close friendship during my time as a publisher ran a small store for devotional objects and religious books in secularized Berlin, and I was fascinated and thrilled by the entrepreneurial courage that these young people showed. (Incidentally, Christians were far from their type of customers.)

At the time, they were celebrating the tenth anniversary of their shop's existence, and they were rightfully proud. I offered to honor their anniversary by celebrating a Mass in their store, to which they could invite friends and clients. They accepted enthusiastically, and it was a great celebration—but when I think back on it, it was certainly somewhat too big, on my part. A prayer, a moment of reflection, or a meditation would have been just as fitting. But no, I wanted to give it my all and to give the best I could, to celebrate the Eucharist. However, the Eucharist wasn't quite suited to the "target audience," because most of the customers had no experience whatsoever with the Eucharist. Today I might select a more appropriate form. But my naivete and my friendship with the family protected me and all the other participants and made everything work in the end.

I tell this story to encourage you to let out your missionary energy if it grips you, even if it may seem to be "too much" at times. For example, we know that converted people or those who have had their faith reawakened are especially missionary. That makes sense. They want to share what moved them to their conversion. Of course, one should find the appropriate measure as well. But the petrifying timidity that counts as political correctness these days has nothing to do with the gospel. By holding back, we sin more against ourselves than we might harm others through our show of faith.

If we want to relearn how to express ourselves, how to go outside ourselves—and not only in questions of faith—then we need to overcome our fear of being inappropriate. I can only find out what is inappropriate by speaking, not by holding back. At the end of one of his sermons, Meister Eckhart, the great German mystic of the thirteenth and fourteenth century, once said, "Had there been none here [in the church], I would have had to hold the sermon to the offertory box."[2] The learned mystic simply had to let it out—so let us let it out, as well!

Jesus is familiar with this feeling, too. In the Gospel of Luke, we read, "At daybreak he departed and went into a deserted place. And the crowds were looking for him; and when they reached him, they wanted to prevent him from leaving them. But he said to them, 'I must proclaim the good news of the kingdom of God to the other cities also; for I was sent for this purpose.' So he continued proclaiming the message in the synagogues of Judea" (4:42-44). When it comes to faith, there is something in us that cannot be stopped. If we try to hold it back, we do ourselves and God—and everyone else, for that matter—no favors. In his *Confessions*, St. Augustine writes a great deal about his conversion. In one case, he writes, "But how does one talk about you (God)? Woe to those who are silent about you, for even the dumb shall confess you."[3] When we open our mouths to talk about faith, we are worried that we might annoy others or intrude too deeply into their privacy. In a dialogue sermon on world missionary day in Leipzig, religion teacher Regina Nothelle and judge Sabine Zarden reflected on this exact topic:

But why missionize at all? Isn't everyone free to believe in whatever way they want? Most people either have some sort of belief with which they are happy or at least live comfortably. Or alternatively, they consciously choose not to have anything to do with God and the Church. In that case, they are happy and satisfied because of that very choice. But are they really? And isn't it just a different kind of condescension to over-zealously respect others' beliefs? If I use conversation or, maybe even better, my way of life to introduce someone to an alternative to their prior convictions or lifestyle—without any pressure or force—then they have the option of deciding freely. If I say nothing, I'm not even offering a choice, I'm in fact denying that they have the competence to choose according to the facts of the case.[4]

5

# THE MISSIONARY SPIRIT

There are other missionaries besides Christian missionaries. For example, many people see it as their mission to eat no meat—on the one hand, because it is healthy, and on the other hand, because they are convinced that the only way the world can survive is if we reduce our consumption of meat. Others take to the streets to protest global social injustices. Whatever they do, it is fueled by the wish to make the world better. Some are even convinced that without these changes, the world has no future. In Judeo-Christian terms, one could say that these people have discovered the prophetic part of themselves.

"Don't take yourself so seriously" is a now famous dictum by Pope John XXIII, showing the serenity and trust in God he radiated. Paradoxically, it was this very same serenity and trust, rather than his missionary fervor, that helped him initiate something truly major, the Second Vatican Council. In doing so, he opened the whole Church, not just its windows and doors, to the world. The missionary is tempted to want to save the world or the Church. That's only natural; it's hard to bear witness without identifying strongly with something. If one does not identify strongly with something, there is no motivation to go outside oneself and become vulnerable by approaching others. That can go as far as the missionary seeing himself as being equivalent to the message and on one level with the one who sent him. He feels that unless *he* does or says something, no one will. But God knows many ways and can find other paths, as well. This kind of missionary zeal can be dangerous.

The "missionary spirit" is human. Everybody has some mission, or even several missions. And just as this gift can be used for one's own good and that of humanity, it can also become dangerous. It is a common temptation to paint first a damning picture of the world, and then emphasize the need for salvation much more strongly. But this is not in the spirit of the Gospels. Jesus was never disrespectful of the world. Even as he saw its need for help and salvation, he always saw goodness at its core. Why should God have wanted to become man if the world and all earthly things are evil?

Demonizing the world can also extend to demonizing people in general or specific groups of people. When we do that, we summon up the devil rather than casting him out. In the Christian view, the world has already been saved through Jesus Christ (see Rev 1:5). Nothing need be added. Jesus is searching for workers in the continual building of God's kingdom, but it remains God's kingdom. Believing that I can or must save the world is blasphemy. It makes no sense to praise Christ as the one who has saved us and simultaneously give the impression (and believe) that without me (or without the Church) all is lost. "I think the Christians would have to look more saved. They should have to sing better songs to me if I were to believe in their savior," as the pastor's son and atheist Friedrich Nietzsche put it. And even if I don't *look* saved, I can believe that I have been saved.

## WHAT IS SUCCESS?

Often, it is especially the people who do volunteer work or who work professionally at spreading the faith who are frustrated when they don't see success in their efforts. Jesus gives his disciples a parable that may comfort us in this context: the parable of the seed and the sower. We can assume that Jesus is referring to his own experience of spreading the faith, too, when he tells the parable of the sower:

> That same day Jesus went out of the house and sat beside the sea. Such great crowds gathered around him that he got into a boat and sat there, while the whole crowd stood on the beach. And he told them many things in parables, saying: "Listen! A sower went out to sow. And as he sowed, some seeds fell on the path, and the birds came and ate them up. Other seeds fell on rocky ground, where they did not have much soil, and they sprang up quickly, since they had no depth of soil. But when the sun rose, they were scorched; and since they had no root, they withered away. Other seeds fell among thorns, and the thorns grew up and choked them. Other seeds fell on good soil and brought forth grain, some a hundredfold, some sixty, some thirty. Let anyone with ears listen!" (Matt 13:1–9)

Jesus spreads the word of God on the mount, in the temple, when he is passing, to the sick, to his disciples, to anyone in earshot. He is constantly "sowing." But the acceptance of the Word is not in his hands, just as the sower has no control over his own success. Missionary work is primarily sowing. A friend of mine who is a pastor in a much-secularized context once told me that he has often lovingly prepared sermons or events for his congregation, but only a handful of people come. He is understandably disappointed when he asks, "My parish consists of several thousand members, so why do only six people show up?" He was certain that it could not be the quality of the events. One day, he hit upon the solution to the problem: "As long as I see myself literally as a 'pastor,' as the shepherd of the flock whose size I know and for whom I feel responsible, I'm going to be frustrated, because I'm always counting backward. How many are missing from a hundred percent? But if I see myself as a missionary, I can be happy about every single person who comes. Whether it's two, three, or four, everyone who comes is a gain and a success."

Jesus once said, "For where two or three are gathered in my name, I am there among them" (Matt 18:20). That's humble, at least regarding quantity in real numbers. But missionaries are wasteful. They spread seed everywhere, and if some of it falls on rocky ground, so what? Missionaries are only being as wasteful as God himself is. Was God stingy when he made the world? Missionaries are as wasteful as nature, too, which doesn't stint in the number of seeds it spreads. At the same time, Jesus is no stranger to these missionary impulses. There are so many passages showing him distraught about the "lack of success" of his mission: "But to what will I compare this generation? It is like children sitting in the marketplaces and calling to one another, 'We played the flute for you, and you did not dance; / we wailed, and you did not mourn'" (Matt 11:16–17). But the reason for this sadness was not his own ego that had specific expectations. Instead, it was the fact that God could not (yet) reach his people.

We may sow the seeds, but it is God who lets things grow. And the recipient of the message is responsible for where the seed falls. The parable of the sower begins with a clear distance between Jesus and the listeners: he is standing in a boat; they are at the shore. It isn't our responsibility how the Word is received. But if the sower constantly holds on to the seeds—wants to control the outcome of his preaching—then there is no chance that they will fall on fertile ground. We need to let go.

One reason that we sometimes feel frustrated when we look at our mission today and see how little our efforts yield (they may not even bear fruit in us) may be that we remember the "glorious" nineteenth century, probably *the* century for missionary work. It is in that century that many of the missionary orders, such as the Comboni Missionaries, the Society of the Divine Word, the Missionaries of the Sacred Heart, the Missionary Benedictines, and so on, were founded. And they went out into the entire world, to all the continents, and spread the gospel with (largely) remarkable success. All the while, the missionary fervor working at home strengthened this trend. We find none of this today.

But we should be humble in our expectations. If we follow Jesus' parable, then our "success rate," and that of Jesus himself, will be only 25 percent. After all, only one quarter of the grain falls on fertile soil. Just as the seed is God's word and does not belong to us, the reason why the word bears fruit sometimes and not at others is hidden from us as well. For example, I know a few families in which one child is particularly pious and engaged in religious matters. But in the same family, there is generally also another, different child who wants nothing to do with faith, despite the familial closeness. Sometimes I think that there's a sense in it for both sides: the faithful are a thorn in the side of the atheist; and the atheist in the side of the religious person.

Can we even really judge what "success" in testifying means? Is it the numbers at all? We may not even see success when it is right in front of us. We may not see it *yet*, because growth takes time. All in all, Jesus' parable tells us, we shouldn't think too much about success but instead focus on our part: sowing the seed.

Farmers and gardeners need patience. The priest in my home parish once told me,

> I'm still happy when I think back to one young woman in my congregation. At the age of sixteen, she asked to be baptized, and after a period of preparation and conversation, I baptized her during the Easter eve service. Four years later, I met her in the city, and she told me, "That baptism was the right choice and the most beautiful thing in my life." As a priest, that conversation did me such good because, particularly with young people, we often think we're putting in so much effort for nothing. It seems like after they receive the sacrament, that's it. But this case showed me that I need to keep sowing generously because I can't be sure on what ground the seed will bear fruit. I shouldn't underestimate the power of my life and my work. In a society, too, that is distancing itself from faith and religion more and more, there is still a soul somewhere that is searching and needs me, as a priest.

Sowing means hoping.

## SETTING THE BAR

Volkenroda monastery in Germany's Thuringia region is the site of the impressive "Christus Pavilion," which was originally built for the Expo 2000 in Hanover. The Pavilion is open to all confessions, and unlike in many traditional churches, there are no steps leading up to the church space from the surrounding ground. This is meant to express the idea that accessing Christ should be as easy as possible for all people. There are no obstacles, so that you can't develop "threshold anxiety"; in fact, there's not even a threshold. The other side of this coin is that I have sometimes seen tourists simply ride their bicycles straight into the space—and who can blame them? Since they had no experience of sacred spaces, they had no natural feeling of awe and respect and thought one could simply ride in on one's bike. That is very nearly disrespect. In pastoral care, "low-threshold" events are those that are designed to allow people with no or little religious background to get in touch with a spiritual experience. One example from the United States is "theology on tap," where people get together in a bar and talk about their faith. For many people, meeting up in a bar is easier than going straight to a church or to a parish hall. Many monasteries and dioceses also hold concerts: Music is one of the wonderful ways of letting others experience God. First and foremost, it is art, and the listeners can decide for themselves whether they want to consider the explicitly religious implications. Such offers are great.

Especially when encountering people who don't bring much personal religious experience to the table, one should be careful to use "low-threshold" language. It makes no sense to keep tossing out terms from the Bible or from dogmatics when the other person cannot connect with or understand them. Furthermore, religious speech has often been misused in the past, and people may associate certain expressions with painful memories, such as terrifying religious education classes. This is one of the reasons why, after the Second Vatican Council, there was a conscious "disarmament" and a search to find words that would describe spiritual ideas in more neutral, "worldly" ways. But there are negative sides and limits to what this can do. It seems appropriate and justified when we are speaking to people who have experienced some elements of religious education. They can take in and understand such language. But when people know or understand nothing at all about religion, they will not even understand my "low-threshold" language. In those cases, I can introduce a religious term or two, which can then become a starting point for talking about them. If the terms spark a question or surprise in the person I am talking to, that may be my chance to talk about my experiences or to inspire an experience in the other.

Sometimes it's better not to make things too easy. Especially the younger generation, which hasn't had many experiences of the Church, isn't helped much by "softened" language precisely *because* it has had few experiences of the Church. They want to know what we Christians call things. And they want to understand what it means. They want to know precisely. They don't need to be given the freedom to accept or reject it—they take that freedom anyway. Instead, the "low threshold" can lead to a dilution of faith, which helps no one. Or it becomes pandering, which tends to frighten others off.

With people who share my faith, it can indeed be good and helpful to use a kind of "intra-corporate lingo." It's affirming, and it helps not to have to explain to everyone what it means. When the time is right, I can do just that. But I'm also allowed to move within this "company lingo." I remember that I always had great difficulty reading the early Church fathers, such as Augustine or Gregory the Great. It seemed that they simply put one biblical quotation next to another, which I felt was not only outmoded but downright unhelpful. Their language was hermetic. I didn't yet know their scriptural references or was unfamiliar with them, so I had little access to the experience that the respective Church father wanted to describe. After years, or more accurately, decades of study and reading of Scripture, however, these texts—which weren't originally intended for specialists but were still heard by people who were continually educating themselves about and with the Bible—make a different kind of sense. They are extremely affirming, logically rigorous, and healing. So why dilute the things that are truly nutritious? We can trust people with not necessarily understanding everything at first glance. We can leave the thresholds where they are, so that people can't immediately come in: a threshold can become an incentive to work, which is often more motivating than an attempt to make everything more transparent—particularly when those things cannot be made immediately transparent.

In other words, if we lower the barriers in religious matters to their lowest level, people cannot grow. It's okay not to understand something occasionally. There's no sense in trivializing the divine. However, the words I choose, how high I make the threshold, should be based entirely on the person I encounter. Love and respect should guide my choice of words. It has simply been my experience that sometimes a higher threshold can be a better way to show the other something of my faith.

6

# OUR RELATIONSHIP WITH THE CHURCH

For many, their relationship with the Church can be a barrier to bearing witness. This is a shame, because the Church should seek to support us in the witness that we bear.

There are many who have made their break with the Church or who have simply grown out of it while still believing in God or in Christ, and any avowal to God or Christ makes our world better. Many others, however, feel connected to the Church, but have problems with one or two or even many people in or representing it. This is particularly painful since it is so much easier to bear witness if we can fully identify with our faith community. So, it makes sense to work positively on our relationship with the Church. But what is my understanding of Church? For me, the following images have become important.

Far beyond the church as an institution subject to temporal constraints, the Church is also the Body of Christ. St. Paul the Apostle uses this image: "For just as the body is one and has many members, and all the members of the body, though many, are one body, so it is with Christ. For in the one Spirit we were all baptized into one body" (1 Cor 12:12–13). This means that we should represent, present, demonstrate Christ in this world. "Christ has no hands but ours," says a prayer from the early fourteenth century. Seeing oneself as a limb, or member, of his body, one becomes conscious of our limitations as a human being. This, in turn, makes me kinder toward the other limbs, the other members of the Church, whether at its base or top or middle. With our limited human means, we are all trying to let some of Christ's goodness, kindness, and clarity shine through.

This approach helps me not to despair when I have grievances with the Church or I see things going in what I feel to be the wrong direction. This attitude also prevents anger, bitterness, or disappointment taking control of my relationship with the Church. The thought makes me humble: I am only a single limb. I need to respect the others, too. "If the foot would say, 'Because I am not a hand, I do not belong to the body,' that would not make it any less a part of the body" (1 Cor 12:15). On the contrary, holding the tension that I experience when I don't fully identify can be a fruitful contribution to the Church. If I leave the Church, I no longer contribute to it. Feeling with the Church (sentire cum ecclesia—Ignatius of Loyola) includes both joy and suffering. I am joyful about the new pope, but I also suffer about one thing or another. Many things regarding the Church come and go; Christ remains the same. It is about him and his message. Certainly, concentrating on the essentials makes sense, especially in times of change, whether they be moral or dogmatic questions. There is a kind of "hierarchy of truths." The Church does not require some sort of authoritarian submission in the form of complete identification with every single one of its smallest claims. Above all, we are united by central truths of faith, such as Christ's resurrection. Questions of contraception, for example, are important, but do not have the same level of significance.

Over the years, we ourselves change and begin to see things differently. The Church's store of faith contains the larger whole, some of which we cannot always immediately understand or assent to. It also includes the entire world with all its cultures. Christian life does not consist in memorizing everything like some model pupil only to know and parrot it back. We are talking about a mystery, the "mystery of faith." We are talking about Jesus' life, death, and resurrection. Who can honestly say they have understood that? Who truly believes it on every level? Humility in this area is only appropriate—and it makes our lives easier.

I am both astounded and grateful for the fact that over the years, I "understand" more and more of the Bible and the teachings of the Church. I marvel that I can recognize how so many things fit together, how wisely they are joined. Perhaps not all things, but then the Church is constantly working at itself, as we have seen in the last fifty years. But I also must admit that I simply didn't use to understand many things when I was younger, despite being socialized in a religious environment and studying theology. I was simply not far enough along in my personal development to be able to understand them. I am so grateful to the Church, that is, to my brothers and sisters, for continuing to carry the whole faith during this time. And I am overjoyed at the thought of how much more and how much more deeply I have yet to understand. "O the depth of the riches and wisdom and knowledge of God! How unsearchable are his judgments and how inscrutable his ways! 'For who has known the mind of the Lord? / Or who has been his counselor?' / 'Or who has given a gift to him, / to receive a gift in return?' / For from him and through him and to him are all things. To him be the glory forever. Amen" (Rom 11:33–36).

Humility is also appropriate because we are not bearing witness only to the faith of billions of others all over the world but also to the things our forefathers experienced with God. This history is part of the rich store of our faith because we believe that God interacted with our mothers and fathers in the same way as he is doing with us today. At our core, I believe that we humans don't change all that much over the ages, even if the digital revolution, climate change, and globalization can sometimes appear as though humanity was fundamentally altered. Missionaries simply used to go out and spread what "was Catholic." In a way, they had an easier time. As individuals, they were able to hide behind the collective. Today, the individual is back at the forefront. But having to carve every religious experience out of the wood of my own life is not only inappropriate, it is expecting too much of myself. Why not trust in our forefathers, at least as much as we can trust in ourselves?

Regarding evangelization, the Church has the advantage that it has our back—we are not alone and we are not the only ones who believe or have experienced these crazy things. By sending the disciples out two by two, Jesus enshrined the missionary work of the Church in its very beginnings. The Church has a kind of "hive intelligence," and over the centuries it has developed mechanisms of recognizing and correcting the dangers of both the collective and the individual. For example, the Church is critical of private revelations: it is the congregation or the collective that decides what is believable—as in Jesus' times.

So, when I bear witness, I should actively understand myself as part of the Church. That means that I should first apply anything that I accuse the Church of—large or small, rightly or wrongly—to myself. The Church is too exclusionary. Am *I* too exclusionary? The Church is hypocritical. Am *I* hypocritical, or do my actions and my words match? The Church is authoritarian. How much freedom do *I* grant others in their thoughts and their actions?

We cannot separate Church and faith, because the nature of the Christian faith is communal: it is passed on by telling our stories. At Pentecost, the moment the Church was "born," this feeling of being one—despite being so many and so different—

was the Holy Spirit being poured out, sending out all the disciples and giving them the courage to bear witness. Each one of us is a part of that Spirit, just as the flame appeared above the heads of all disciples. The Holy Spirit, in the end, is indivisible, and the experience of Pentecost makes sense only if it kindles and constitutes a community.

This unification is incredibly important when bearing witness. If I am not one with myself, I am not a credible witness. If the Church is not one, it too isn't credible, which is why we should work as ecumenically as possible. Far more things unite us than separate us. We have reached a point in our society in which the Christian faith threatens to evaporate completely. We cannot afford to be schismatic, separated. We can see this in the graying heads in the church pews. What used to be the "Christian West" need not remain Christian just because it is full of churches that are these days used more for other purposes than for services. The best example of this is North Africa, which was deeply Christian until the seventh century. Or Asia Minor, modern-day Turkey, which was also Christian, but no longer is. As ever, Pope Francis finds clear words in this respect. In his message at World Mission Day in 2013, he emphasized that Church work is teamwork:

> It is urgent in our time to announce and witness to the goodness of the Gospel, and this from within the Church itself. It is important never to forget a fundamental principle for every evangelizer: one cannot announce Christ without the Church. Evangelization is not an isolated individual or private act; it is always ecclesial. Paul VI wrote, "When an unknown preacher, catechist or Pastor, preaches the Gospel, gathers the little community together, administers a Sacrament, even alone, he is carrying out an ecclesial act." He

acts not "in virtue of a mission which he attributes to himself or by a personal inspiration, but in union with the mission of the Church and in her name" (*Evangelii Nuntiandi*, 60). And this gives strength to the mission and makes every missionary and evangelizer feel never alone, but part of a single Body animated by the Holy Spirit.[1]

In every context, it is useful first to talk about the good experiences we have had with the Church—because we all have had good experiences, otherwise we would no longer belong to the Church. We shouldn't let our general approval be darkened by the classic topics of disagreement. Neither, though, should we try to avoid these topics if they come up in discussion.

## BEING CHOSEN

In the New York Holocaust Museum, there is footage of a survivor recounting a particularly inescapable situation in the camps. Certain he was going to die, he started to pray, though he had never been a particularly observant Jew: "Why, God, do you let all this happen? We are your chosen people!"

Many people may bridle at this idea of being "chosen by God." We're suspicious of the idea. Too many evils have been done in the name of "chosenness," particularly by Christians to Jews. But this testimony by the Holocaust survivor struck me deep in my heart. "We are your chosen people!" What dignity comes from these words. Let's consider the claim from a different perspective. When a man loves a woman, the woman, too, is indescribably happy at having been "chosen," and vice versa, of course. But there are many other women as well. She may ask, "Why has the man chosen *me*?" There are also many other men. So, the man may ask, "Why does she love me in particular?" Love and chosenness go hand in hand.

From the beginning, the people of Israel have felt that they were chosen by God and have a unique relationship in the world. It was a small group, quite "downtrodden," living in Egypt as slaves. But its faith in its chosenness helped it stand up and free itself. Being chosen by God means something different from being chosen by a person such as a husband. God's choice is exclusive, while not cutting out anyone else. Like a good mother or a good father, he can love all his children while also loving each of his children completely. This is the kind of chosenness we are talking about. Young Christians soon adopted this idea of the "chosen people" of Israel. The Church saw itself as a "new Israel," especially chosen and blessed by God. This idea asserts that the deepest faith is rooted in the Church, that God will never desert the Church on its path through the ages. It will not fall, no matter what it encounters. Even the Old Testament uses the image of the lover: God as the lover of Israel. The Church is simply continuing the thought: it considers itself the "bride" of Christ. Both are inseparably linked and meant for one another.

But the Church has always thought that what is true of the congregation of the faithful is true of everyone as well: every Christian is connected with Christ in the unbreakable bond of baptism. Every one of us is chosen, every one of us intended. All of us are loved, and we all have a mission. No one can be left out. If you let this thought enter deep into your heart, it gives joy, an immense peace, and meaning to your life.

When I encounter a person whom I want to tell about my faith, I can't walk around with an attitude of "I've been chosen!" But I can keep that thought in the back of my mind and use it as a resource for myself. At the same time, I'm being challenged actively to believe that God has chosen and loves the person I'm talking to in the same exclusive way. In the Gospel according to John, Jesus reminds us, "You did not choose me but I chose you. And I appointed you to go and bear fruit, fruit that will last, so that the Father will give you whatever you ask him in my name" (John 15:16). The First Epistle of Peter confirms this idea: "But you are a chosen race, a royal priesthood, a holy nation, God's own people, in order that you may proclaim the mighty acts of him who called you out of darkness into his marvelous light" (1 Pet 2:9).

## COOPERATIVE AND SUPPORTIVE

Each of us is chosen to be part of the congregation of the faithful with our own specific mission in the total plan. Each of us plays a significant role no one else can fulfill. Spreading the gospel is a communal task. Charismatic individual preachers may contribute, but in the end, it is the community that proves convincing (or unconvincing). This has been standard practice for missionary monasteries from the very beginning, as our monastery demonstrates. When our mission was directed solely at people in Africa and Asia, about a third of our monks were "outside" in the world, preaching the gospel in developing countries and helping to build the infrastructure. The rest stayed in the home Abbey of Münsterschwarzach, being supportive: materially, by making or repairing items; financially, by collecting donations; and spiritually, by writing letters or dedicating prayers. One prayed for the mission. And when the missionaries came home on leave, everything was done to make sure they could recover their strength.

Other confreres in Münsterschwarzach worked in fundraising for the mission. The monastery's workshops made special items for the mission. The school was called a "mission seminary" and had the goal of educating future missionaries. Each classroom had a small box in which the students could place their donations for the mission. The monks distributed (and sometimes still distribute) calendars describing the mission. In short, everyone contributed to the missionary project. It was a communal effort, and every monk saw it as his highest goal to be sent on a mission outside the monastery. But, as I've said, only a small number of monks could be sent out, as the rest were needed at home. There, too, monks were fulfilled because they were supporting the mission "on the home front." Even today, it is characteristic of Benedictines to see their missionary work as communal work. In doing so, they are trying to live by the principles that structure the entire Church.

When a community has a mission, it has an identity. It knows its purpose, and its members know its purpose. This is important in a monastery because it allows energies to be combined and directed effectively. "Idleness is the enemy of the soul," writes St. Benedict.[2]

When I asked a young confrere, what was the most beautiful thing he had experienced as a missionary, he answered, "The community." When we contribute to a mission, we experience the Holy Spirit and that community. Those are deeply fulfilling experiences. When we missionize as a community, we are not only more effective but also more authentic. We come closer to the vision God has for this world. God wants to make a "new heaven and a new earth," a "new Jerusalem" (Rev 21:1–2). The image that St. John's Revelation chooses for God's kingdom is the city, the place where people can live together in peace. If we bear witness to our faith together, people can read in us how that might be possible. St. Benedict built his monastery, Montecassino, atop a high mountain so that it could be seen from all around. At the end of his rule, he writes of his monks,

"They should value nothing whatever above Christ himself, and may he bring us all together to eternal life."[3] For him, eternal life is a communal project, not something that individuals can attain or deserve. In that sense, there is no one missionary, but only the team, the community, the group of missionizers.

Maybe you can apply this idea to your own situation. Isn't it easier to approach people together, and especially people on the margins—immigrants in our neighborhoods, old people who are socially isolated, the terminally or chronically ill, people who have lost hope because they have lost the source of their faith? After all, communal prayer also gives us greater joy than individual prayer; you can't really have a party of one. Though there is much discussion about the meaning and the future of "the congregation," I believe that there is no alternative to its structure.

The division of labor, then, is a characteristic of mission work—and not just of the actual missionizing: it also includes praying for missionaries. One might ask what Jesus was doing after he had sent out his disciples. We don't have any record of it, but we can easily imagine that he was praying for his apostles. "I watched Satan fall from heaven like a flash of lightning" (Luke 10:18), he tells them when they return. How could he have seen that if his thoughts had not been with his disciples?

This contemplative function "in the background" of missionary work (or maybe even in the foreground, who knows?) is epitomized in the life of St. Thérèse of Lisieux (1873–97), which is probably why Pope Pius XI named her patron saint of world missions even though, as a cloistered Carmelite nun, she saw very little of the world herself. But in prayer, she crossed borders for the missionaries. There is a letter by St. Thérèse in which she writes to Fr. Adolphe Roulland about his missionary work and states that she hopes for her support to extend beyond the missionaries she touches directly. In heaven, she writes, she will remain Fr. Roulland's "Little Sister," and indeed their connection will become even closer, as her soul will transcend cloisters and fly to the furthest missionary destinations—while his tools of the apostolate will remain his, so will prayer remain her weapon in mission.

Supporting one another is another key role for the congregation of the faithful. An African priest who ministers to a German congregation once told me about an impressive example of this:

> At the beginning of my work, the thing that was probably most important to me was the question of the acceptance of my work and of me as a person in a Church that is informed by over a thousand years of history, culture, and tradition, while my young Church in the Congo is only a hundred years old. Now, half a year before my 'silver anniversary' as a priest, I look back on sixteen beautiful and enriching years of priestly work in German churches. And what I—an "imported priest in Germany," as a television documentary once described me—see as the most joyous moments in my life are moments in which I am accepted and in which I have the feeling that I as a priest am needed. There's an example I can use to illustrate this. When in the summer of 2006 my current congregation learned that they were to be given to a priest born in the African Congo, some members of the congregation were not enthusiastic, and some were unwilling to be buried by a black priest. To support me, the deacon decided that no other priest or officiant should take on the burial in such a case. I was only told this story personally several years after

I had become the congregation's minister. It deeply touched and strengthened me and gave me joy. I felt fully accepted by my German confreres and colleagues. I was able to depend on their trust and their help. And indeed, I never had the feeling that I wasn't in the right place. On the contrary, I am a full part of the Church here, and my work is valued.

Missionaries are vulnerable because they are foreign, and so they need someone to have their back. That includes having a place where, as a missionary, one can tell one's story within the family, so to speak. After Jesus had sent out his disciples, he did not become reclusive and refuse to be seen. Instead, he waited for their return (see Luke 10:17). The disciples joyfully began to recount what they had experienced, and those people who go outside themselves and to others experience a great deal. Those experiences aren't always joyful. But it is helpful for the health of one's soul to share such difficult experiences. Bearing witness means going outside oneself, and it is helpful to practice it even within our own communities. For example, these days it is very important for anyone involved in catechetics or religious teaching—and in a certain way, those people are missionaries—to keep looking for times and spaces where they can talk about their experiences. This exchange reduces feelings of disappointment and can present ideas for future projects. All of us need this support.

## BEING OUTSIDERS

Missionaries are "outside." That can result in being cast as an outsider in one's own community, and in feeling like an outsider, as well. Support isn't always perfect, nor can it be. After all, how can people at home be completely understanding of the missionary and his experiences when those experiences are totally new?

This has always been the case in the Church. Let us look at the early Church's most prominent missionaries, Paul and Barnabas. Both are not from the original circle of the twelve apostles, those sent by Jesus himself. They cannot claim to have been part of things from the very beginning (see Acts 1:21-22). But the Lord has appeared to them as well—so they must communicate even more with their brothers and sisters in Jerusalem. They need to talk about what they have experienced on their journey.

This problem has not changed to this day. Missionaries walk the boundaries of the Church itself, and that often makes them pioneers. My brother missionaries in China and Korea celebrated Mass facing the congregation already in the first half of the last century, long before the practice was finally legitimized by the Second Vatican Council. In their encounters with fellow Asian Christians, they realized that God had called them to do this. This realization was probably helped by the fact that they were far away from Rome and didn't yet have Skype or email.

But this example can also show us that the renewal of the Church can often come from its borders, from the "missionary zones." This is natural. The people who come into an existing community bring changes—and thank God for that! A Church that has lost its missionary spirit cannot be renewed.

So, we should not be frustrated if we sometimes feel like outsiders; if we sometimes do or experience things that aren't accepted or understood by the whole community of the faithful at home. It is the task of those who remain home to keep the faith. It is the task of those who go out to spread and to broaden the faith.

In a certain way, the missionary's task is the more demanding one. Paul, for example, must pay a literal price in the Jerusalem congregation for allowing new non-Jewish Christians to remain uncircumcised, and does a kind of fundraising drive: "They asked only one thing, that we remember the poor, which was actually what I was eager to do" (Gal 2:10). Missionaries are in a position of obligation. Since they are on unfamiliar territory, they cannot expect the people back home to accept everything immediately. They must actively search for contact with "central command" and the establishment at home. In effect, they must simultaneously missionize outward and inward.

## ASKING THE RIGHT QUESTIONS

When we show our faith, we enter a situation of communication. There is a *sender*, a *receiver*, and *content* that is communicated. From communication theory, we know that this content depends largely on the way we communicate it. In other words: *what* the other person says is almost irrelevant. The thing that reaches me first and foremost is *how* he says it. The nonverbal part of communication (i.e., the things that I don't say but still communicate and project) shape the conversation. That's why it is so important for my conversation partner to experience me as an open, friendly person. We may be more convincing if we smile at someone or make an inviting gesture, or when we share our joy during cooking or sports. "Come and see," says Jesus and invites the disciples into his home (see John 1:39). See how I live.

Of course, content is important as well. *How* I believe is not the only important thing, but *what* I believe. Both, *fides quae* and *fides qua*, have always had a high degree of importance in the Christian tradition. In a way, the content of our faith is always part of the *how*. We don't teach just anything. There is objective content, an objective truth: God loves us; he created this earth; he sent us his Son; God became man; he proclaimed God's kingdom and lived it for us; he loved us so much that he even suffered for us and died for us. In so doing, he restored our relationship with God and purged our sins, once and for all; he conquered death; he was not deserted by God but resurrected by him; he lives, even today; he appeared to the disciples, so he can also appear to us; in baptism, he opens the gates to eternal life. The Church proclaims this joyous news and tries to realize it in its communities. More and more, I am losing my fear of talking about the content of my faith, completely apart from cultivating an open, advertising attitude. What we believe matters, and it is not of secondary importance. It may come second in the sense of communication theory, but it is not secondary in our faith.

Our faith finds its beginning in a very specific occurrence: the resurrection of Jesus Christ. Pope Benedict XVI once described the resurrection as the beginning of a new era. In a lecture to American abbots, the theologian and Benedictine monk Jeremy Driscoll explained why Jesus' resurrection must also be the cornerstone of all efforts of evangelization: Jesus' explicit mission to his disciples (see Matt 28:18-20) began after the resurrection—and thus presupposes and requires it.

Jesus' death confronts us with three urgent questions:

1. Who is God that he permits the death of his Son?

2. Who is Jesus that he willingly walks into this death instead of fleeing from it?

3. Who are the disciples that they must stand by and witness this senseless death?

For three days, the disciples are left alone with these questions, not knowing whether they will ever find a compelling answer to them. But they receive one on Easter morning:

1. God is the one who never deserts his Son or any of his sons and daughters, who instead rescues them from death.

2. Jesus is the one who was resurrected from the dead by God.

3. The disciples are the ones who bear witness to this resurrection.

Bearing witness, then, begins at the empty grave. No mission without Easter. Our task, of course, is not to let the interpersonal level be overshadowed by the content level, whether in our catechetics, our religious teachings, our Sunday schools, or our conversations with our own children and grandchildren. That used to be the case much more so than now. The content was "beaten into" young people—sometimes literally—which left many wounds that are still painful.

However, a total focus on authenticity and total adaptation to the subjective standards of a given target group has just as little to do with spreading the gospel. Here, the pendulum has certainly swung too far back to the other side. My experience has always been that the less people know about the content of Christian teaching, the more eagerly they listen when I try to find the words to tell them about it.

The content of our revelation is in fact simple and short. (The many additions came later and have different amounts of relevance.) Paul sums up the message:

> For I handed on to you as of first importance what I
> in turn had received: that Christ died for our sins in

accordance with the scriptures, and that he was bur-
ied, and that he was raised on the third day in accordance with the scriptures, and that he appeared to
Cephas, then to the twelve. Then he appeared to
more than five hundred brothers and sisters at one
time, most of whom are still alive, though some have
died. Then he appeared to James, then to all the
apostles. Last of all, as to one untimely born, he
appeared also to me. For I am the least of the apostles, unfit to be called an apostle, because I persecuted the church of God. (1 Cor 15:3-9)

If we proclaim Christ without faith in the resurrection, he
is a spiritual teacher like any other. Certainly, a very good and
impressive one, but also interchangeable. We will then lose the
energy and motivation to go outside ourselves and talk about
faith at all, however—for why should we, if he is just another
teacher? The historical event of Jesus' death and resurrection
set everything in motion and continues to set everything in
motion—even today.

The three days of unanswered questioning are also important for us as disciples today. We must give one another time to
understand the contents of our faith from within, just as God
gave the disciples time back then. Time for doubt, uncertainty,
and searching—those times belong to our faith as well. Instead
of giving answers right away, in conversations about faith it can
sometimes be better just to ask questions, questions that open
a space in which answers can grow.

# 7

# RETURNING HOME TO CHRIST

These final chapters will address those who want to live their lives out of a greater identification with the Church and with faith, whether professionally or in their private lives. Consequently, some of the vocabulary may be "too steep a climb" for "beginners." So, whatever may seem too difficult or too far from your experience you can discard, but the things that seem helpful you may carry with you.

Passing on our faith begins in Jesus and finds its completion in him as well. Just as the disciples set out from him and return to him again, our heart, when it has gone out and transcended, is invited to return home to Jesus. If we believe that Christ lives in every person, then we have already come home whenever we encounter him in our fellow human beings. Each time we bear witness must always be radically Christ-centered. Cardinal Timothy Dolan of New York once described this, saying, "A third necessary ingredient in the recipe of effective mission is that God does not satisfy the thirst of the human heart with a proposition, but with a Person, whose name is Jesus. The invitation implicit in the *Missio ad gentes* and the New Evangelization is not to a doctrine but to know, love, and serve—not a something, but a Someone."[1]

However long he traveled and however much he experienced, the Apostle Paul's missionary activity always fed from the intimate relationship he had with Christ. His love for Christ was so strong that it resulted in a mystical union: "It is no longer I who live, but it is Christ who lives in me. And the life I now live in the flesh I live by faith in the Son of God, who loved me and gave himself for me" (Gal 2:20). Paul sees himself as taken fully by Christ and into Christ (see Phil 3:12).

The theology of John the Evangelist knows this heartfelt relationship as well—he lay at Jesus' breast at the Last Supper and was the one to whom Jesus entrusted his mother. He recounts these words: "I am the vine, you are the branches. Those who abide in me and I in them bear much fruit, because apart from me you can do nothing" (John 15:5). Missionary fruitfulness is possible only in intimate union with Christ.

## THE PRICE

So far, we have not really talked about the price of passing on our faith. We have meditated on how encountering others in questions of faith can enrich both sides—and in most cases, that's what happens. But it isn't always so joyful. That may be what Jesus was alluding to when he said, "I am sending you out like lambs into the midst of wolves" (Luke 10:3). Even if I approach another person in a friendly way, unarmed and vulnerable as a lamb, I can sometimes encounter unwillingness or even aggression. Jesus is not naive. He has prepared his disciples for this. There are different degrees of rejection, and it is good for us to keep these gradients in mind, so as not to fall reflexively into an "attitude of martyrdom" if we are rejected. Broadly, there is *ignoring*, *discriminating*, and *persecuting*.

Ignoring is a passive form of aggression. The addressee does not say, "No, that does nothing for me," but he nevertheless lets us feel that he does not support what we've said. He may show this by wrinkling his nose or by simply walking away.

That can be unpleasant, but it should not trouble us further. This is the time to wipe the dust off our feet.

Discrimination, however, is a more grievous form of rejection. For example, someone who knows about my religious convictions refuses to give me a job even though I am qualified for it. This is the reality in China, where Catholics are subject to broad discrimination. In East Germany, too, it was common to shut out Catholics and other Christians who took their faith "too seriously" from forms of higher education, and so on. In Turkey, it is nearly impossible to build churches, and seminaries remain closed. Christians there must accept such discriminatory treatment.

Persecution, finally, is the harshest situation one can encounter as a Christian who proclaims his faith. In our parts of the world, thank God, it is not to be found, but in the rest of the world it is more widespread than we often assume. Today, more Christians are discriminated against, persecuted, and killed than ever before. In its world persecution index, the aid association Open Doors names fifty regions where Christians are persecuted for their beliefs. The situation is worst in Communist North Korea, where Christians are arbitrarily jailed and services are under state surveillance. In addition to imprisonment, the faithful face forced labor and execution, and in countries like Iran, Afghanistan, Saudi Arabia, and even the Maldives, where they routinely oppress Christians, persecution can also lead to death.

People who die because they stood up for their faith are called "martyrs," which translates literally to "blood witnesses." They bear the strongest witness a human being can give. When a person accepts death in order to point to Christ, he or she is in effect saying that Christ means more than one's life. Of course, that makes sense only if one believes in resurrection.

Unfortunately, suicide bombing and other forms of terrorism have given martyrdom a bad name, linking it to people who kill themselves out of religious conviction in the hope of a heavenly reward for killing "infidels" along with them. The Christian martyr has nothing in common with this image. His death is in no way aggressive. It is pure suffering as the consequence of a Christian life. The true martyr, in fact, would rather experience injustice and death than do injustice to anyone else.

The Church remembers the many martyrs throughout its history, but there are also martyrs today. In its yearly report, the Vatican news agency, Agenzia Fides, recounts that over the course of 2012, twelve church employees were murdered: ten priests, one nun, and one layperson.

Missionary work can be life-threatening. The twelve apostles were the first missionaries, and all but one died a violent death for Christ. Jesus had, however, warned them of this possibility: "It is enough for the disciple to be like the teacher, and the slave like the master. If they have called the master of the house Beelzebul, how much more will they malign those of his household!" (Matt 10:25). Jesus himself experienced the most extreme case of what happens when you bear witness. His message and his way of life were rejected; he was sentenced to death and executed. One cannot imagine a more extreme form of rejection.

Jesus was completely authentic. He healed people. He raised people from the dead. And yet he was rejected. It seems that the good news of the coming kingdom of God can include rejection, as well. May God grant that we are never in such a situation as Jesus was—but may he also give us the strength to proclaim our faith and stand for it.

It is about standing for truth, standing for a deeper conviction. No martyr has ever sought martyrdom. Instead, circumstances arose in which believers had the choice of standing by their faith or deserting it. It is a gift to be able to stand by one's faith even in challenging times, and often we don't manage it. Often, we are timid, pussyfooting around questions, just like St. Peter after he has entered the house of the High Priest on the eve of Christ's death. "You also were with Jesus the Galilean," a woman says to him. "I do not know what you are talking about," he replies, denying Jesus out of fear for his own life not once, but three times (Matt 26:69-70).

I have portrayed the extremes of rejection here to encourage us not to lose heart as soon as we encounter even a small amount of resistance. We are doing quite well, after all: religious freedoms in our society have largely been realized. Instead, we're more likely to encounter situations, such as in our jobs, where we might have to speak unpleasant truths and risk detrimental treatment. Looking at the "extreme case" of rejection can teach us what we are called to do in the witness that we bear, which is to stand up for the Truth. When in doubt, we should think more of God and our fellow human beings than of ourselves.

This is another central difference between suicide bombers and Christian martyrs: the latter go to their deaths *for* someone else, in order to give others life. This is exemplified by the Franciscan father Maximilian Kolbe (1894-1941). During the Third Reich, Fr. Kolbe was sent to Auschwitz for publishing Catholic writings in Poland. In the camps, when he saw that sacrificing his own life could save the life of the father of a family, he did not hesitate, but let himself be imprisoned in the starvation bunker. The father survived—Fr. Kolbe had given his life for him.

What is fascinating is that wherever someone gives his life for Christ, an especially ardent veneration of God and spreading of the faith follows. This is the case everywhere on earth, and often the churches have been built on the graves of the martyrs, as in the graves of Sts. Peter and Paul in Rome. But Uganda celebrates its martyrs as well, so does Korea, and so do many other countries. The martyrs' blood is the seed from which new Christians spring forth. It falls onto the earth and bears rich fruit—this is the image the Church uses to explain the inexplicable. The testimony doesn't just work outward, moving people to convert to Christ; it also works inward, strengthening and encouraging the faithful. In the 1950s, two confreres from our monastery were murdered in North Korean concentration camps.[2] This testimony moves our community to this day. In a way, it also gives us a duty: they should not have died in vain.

Generally, the rejection of the messenger does not mean the end of the message. That was true of Christ, and it is true of the Church. In some ways, Christian mission grew out of the persecution of the early Christians! The principle is simple: if we aren't accepted here, we'll go somewhere else—so the persecutors really achieved the opposite of their goal. As Acts relates,

> Thus the word of the Lord spread throughout the region. But the Jews incited the devout women of high standing and the leading men of the city, and stirred up persecution against Paul and Barnabas, and drove them out of their region. So they shook the dust off their feet in protest against them, and went to Iconium. And the disciples were filled with joy and with the Holy Spirit.
>
> The same thing occurred in Iconium, where Paul and Barnabas went into the Jewish synagogue and spoke in such a way that a great number of both Jews and Greeks became believers. (Acts 13:49—14:1)

Martyrdom is a special case of bearing witness, but the principle behind it is at the center of any Christian spirituality. It is about a process that the New Testament calls *kenosis*, meaning an "emptying," "relinquishing," letting go, giving oneself in the way lived out for us by Christ,

> who, though he was in the form of God,
>> did not regard equality with God
>> as something to be exploited,
> but emptied himself,
>> taking the form of a slave,
>> being born in human likeness.
> And being found in human form,
>> he humbled himself
>> and became obedient to the point of death—
>> even death on a cross. (Phil 2:6–8)

If I, too, can make myself "empty" in order to be "filled with God," I become a living sign of God.

Pope John Paul II dedicated one chapter of his encyclical *Redemptoris Missio*[3] to the question of "missionary spirituality." In it, he wrote,

> The mystery of the Incarnation and Redemption is thus described as a total self-emptying which leads Christ to experience fully the human condition and to accept totally the Father's plan. This is an emptying of self which is permeated by love and expresses love. The mission follows this same path and leads to the foot of the cross.
>
> The missionary is required to "renounce himself and everything that up to this point he considered as his own, and to make himself everything to everyone."

[Second Vatican Ecumenical Council, Decree on the Missionary Activity of the Church *Ad Gentes*, 24] This he does by a poverty which sets him free for the Gospel, overcoming attachment to the people and things about him, so that he may become a brother to those to whom he is sent and thus bring them Christ the Savior. This is the goal of missionary spirituality: "To the weak I became weak...; I have become all things to all men, that I might by all means save some. I do it all for the sake of the Gospel..." (1 Cor 9:22–23). (no. 88)

If I "go outside myself" like this, I am abandoning my ego; I am following God's will—no matter the consequences—in the deep faith that God wants what is best for me and all of humanity. When we talk about this kind of spirituality, we often talk about "letting go," or "release," which is exactly what is meant here. By letting go and letting myself fall into God's arms, I am pointing to God, for, as Jesus says, "No one has greater love than this, to lay down one's life for one's friends" (John 15:13).

As Michael Kayoya, a priest from Burundi who was murdered in 1972, stated, "That is what mission is: helping a person, healing him, training him, making him self-assured, educating him, developing the feeling of solidarity in him, making him worthy and free, capable of answering to his eternal purpose. That is mission."

## DON'T WORRY ABOUT WHAT TO SAY

But how should we react when we are rejected for bearing witness—especially when that rejection really pains us, when it is coupled with aggression? First, we can ask ourselves whether there may have been hidden aggression somewhere within our testimony. We can work on getting rid of that part of it. But there may still be cases in which we really did come as "lambs" but received answers from "wolves." What should we do then?

Christian seminaries and theology departments used to teach the discipline of *apologetics*. This subject—known as "fundamental theology" after the Second Vatican Council—probes the foundations of the Christian faith, especially in dialogue with philosophical approaches. In the past, this was a question of "defending" the Christian faith theologically. (*Apologein* means "to defend" in Greek.) I think it makes sense to have good arguments prepared to answer some of the kinds of accusations one faces as a Christian, simply because some of these criticisms repeat or aren't very original. But in the end, the power by which we convince others does not lie on a level on which one can argue or discuss. In the Gospel of Luke, Jesus says, "When they bring you before the synagogues, the rulers, and the authorities, do not worry about how you are to defend yourselves or what you are to say; for the Holy Spirit will teach you at that very hour what you ought to say" (Luke 12:11–12). Why does Jesus recommend this course of action? The beginning of the gospel passage makes it plain: "I tell you, my friends, do not fear those who kill the body, and after that can do nothing more. But I will warn you whom to fear: fear him who, after he has killed, has authority to cast into hell. Yes, I tell you, fear him! Are not five sparrows sold for two pennies? Yet not one of them is forgotten in God's sight. But even the hairs of your head are all counted. Do not be afraid; you are of more value than many sparrows" (Luke 12:4–7).

As soon as our apologetics comes from a place of fear, it no longer has anything to do with the gospel. How can one bear witness to the love of God if one doesn't at that moment deeply believe that God guides and protects one? Any autonomous defense would be a sign of unbelief, and therefore doomed to be ineffective: "So make up your minds not to prepare your defense in advance; for I will give you words and a wisdom that none of your opponents will be able to withstand or contradict" (Luke 21:14–15).

In our hemisphere, one is less likely to encounter direct aggression based on one's religiosity. But passive-aggressiveness is more common. I remember once standing at a passport control at Frankfurt Airport, prior to leaving the country. Unlike on my previous journeys, I was wearing my priest's collar, and after seeing it, the passport officer began to scan the pages of my passport more thoroughly, as if he wanted to check me particularly closely. Until then, I had always experienced passport control as a formality of a few seconds. I had often traveled in and out of the country on this specific passport, as different stamps and visas clearly proved. Nor had the passport expired. Nevertheless, the official thumbed back and forth, until he managed to find something: the passport was missing the seal of the issuing local passport office. No official before him had ever noticed this or mentioned it, but this man told me that because of this, the passport was not valid, and I could not leave the country. I thought this was ridiculous, but—thank God—refrained from saying anything. He left me "in limbo" for a long time, but in the end, I was allowed to pass without any further reason or justification on his part. I believe it was good that I did not let myself be intimidated by his behavior—but also did not defend myself. This made it possible to defuse the situation.

You defend the things you love. If your children were attacked, you would defend them immediately. So, it is an understandable Christian reflex to defend ourselves when someone attacks what we love and value. But it is not always a helpful impulse. By defending ourselves out of fear, we often succeed only in making ourselves weaker and more vulnerable. If, instead, we root ourselves deeply in prayer and faith, we can uphold our testimony. We do not need to defend God. He defends himself. Too much evil has already been done by people trying to defend God. God is much stronger and can do so much better.

But what we can and sometimes must do is to defend *ourselves*. God does not call everyone to martyrdom in every instance. Jesus, after all, also recommended, "Do not give what is holy to dogs; and do not throw your pearls before swine, or they will trample them under foot and turn and maul you" (Matt 7:6). Even if we do not need to defend the sacred, we should at times protect ourselves. Jesus wants what is holy to spread. He does not want us to be extinguished. This is also why it is not always right to show others that which is holy. If we suspect that it might be trampled under the feet of the audience, if we can sense that the other does not have a feeling for the sacred or does not want to have any feeling for Holy-ness, it is better to keep our treasure chest closed. Taking out and displaying our pearls would help neither the audience nor us.

Here, it is appropriate to recall what we noted earlier that when Jesus sends out his disciples, he gives them the following thought for the journey, in case they are rejected:

> But whenever you enter a town and they do not welcome you, go out into its streets and say, "Even the dust of your town that clings to our feet, we wipe off in protest against you. Yet know this: the kingdom of God has come near." I tell you, on that day it will be more tolerable for Sodom than for that town.
>
> Woe to you, Chorazin! Woe to you, Bethsaida! For if the deeds of power done in you had been done in Tyre and Sidon, they would have repented long ago, sitting in sackcloth and ashes. But at the judgment it will

be more tolerable for Tyre and Sidon than for you. And
you, Capernaum,
   will you be exalted to heaven?
     No, you will be brought down to Hades.
"Whoever listens to you listens to me, and whoever rejects you rejects me, and whoever rejects me
rejects the one who sent me." (Luke 10:10–16)

Jesus' calls of woe are difficult to hear, but they do draw
the attention away from us and toward the recipients of the
message and offer of faith. How tragic that these people could
not or would not follow Jesus' call. They harm only themselves
by rejecting an offer of salvation and healing. It will mean their
"woe" when, one day, they look back on their whole lives.

So, the offer of faith should always be kept open. We don't
need to defend the message in and of itself, but sometimes we
do need to defend ourselves. And we are permitted to have pity
for those who have turned against the mercy of God, and we
should pray that one day they can accept God's offer.

# 8

# THE FUNDAMENTALS OF BEING A MISSIONARY

Jesus sends us. This is the reason that we carry his message. It is the deepest and actual motivation for proclaiming our faith. Over the centuries, this calling has expressed itself in diverse ways.[1] In the past centuries, Christian missionaries were driven particularly by the conviction that all people who are not converted and baptized are lost forever. Their main motive was saving souls. They knew that if we do not proclaim God to the people, they are in danger of not being saved and missing their eternal purpose and salvation.

This motivation no longer serves us much. But what are the spiritual motives that might move us today? How can we currently redefine "mission"? There are several possible motivations for mission: offering the faith, offering freedom, being compassionate, awaiting Christ, connecting globally, dialoguing with other religions, and being present. In some ways, these aspects summarize concisely what we have already expressed. They try to realize what Pope John Paul II desired when he coined the term "a new evangelization": it should be "new in its eagerness, in its methods, in its expression."[2]

## OFFERING THE FAITH

"*Propose la foi*," or offering the faith, was the name that French bishops in the year 2000 gave to their new approach toward defining mission in their own country. Now, of course, one can object that this idea makes faith and religion subject to the laws of the market, thereby devaluing them: Christianity as one offer among many! But de facto, that is exactly what it is. And even from a Christian perspective, there can be no other way than to "offer the faith." God's truth may be absolute, but God still offers it to us. Jesus did the same. He never forced anyone to believe. Faith includes a free choice in favor of God, and forcing someone to believe runs contrary to the notion of faith itself. We can read this clearly in Jesus' actions. For example, he leads the Samaritan woman at Jacob's well gently to her own truth, without any moralizing, until she can grasp the Truth—and with it, faith—herself (see John 4:5–42).

This approach frees us from the weight of a misunderstood claim of absoluteness. It makes evangelization easier. We are making an offer of faith. That's all. But that is so much! We are open to the fact of other "service providers in the marketplace" and are open to possible rejection. It is my conviction that this openness does not make the Christian faith weaker, but stronger and more attractive.

When we see faith as an offer, it becomes that much clearer, too, that we need to be guided by the needs of those to whom we make the offer. The first word of St. Benedict's *Rule*, *ausculta*, or "listen,"[3] is also the fundamental attitude of the missionary. He is called to be attentive: What are the desires of the person I am encountering? What does he truly need? Only if I listen and am mindful of the other person can I answer this question honestly.

When I worked as the head of our monastery publishing house, I had to understand economics, which was a sizable leap for someone who had been a theologian, that is, a humanities student. Theologians are more concerned with content than with sales. But in this respect, I have learned a great deal from business. As a good businessperson, I fulfill people's needs, offer them a service they need. To do that, I first need to perceive what their true needs are—churches often answer questions people haven't asked. But how can I fulfill needs by drawing on the treasure of tradition and faith, or by drawing out both the old and the new, as Benedict encourages in his rule? What part of the gospel is particularly healing or desperately needed today? These are the questions we must ask ourselves. The Second Vatican Council programmatically endorsed this approach by stating, "The joys and the hopes, the griefs and the anxieties of the men of this age, especially those who are poor or in any way afflicted, these are the joys and hopes, the griefs and anxieties of the followers of Christ. Indeed, nothing genuinely human fails to raise an echo in their hearts" (*Gaudium et Spes* 1).[4]

I am reminded of the proprietor of a small Lutheran bookstore who spoke in a disparaging tone of the many teachers of a nearby Catholic school who came to her store to buy books. "They just come to me because I'm closer than the Catholic bookshop." So? That is their need: short distances in purchasing devotional literature. They don't have the time to go to the more distant Catholic bookstore. But one is not surprised to learn that the woman soon had to close her bookstore. If I judge the needs of my clients rather than serving them, I won't be very successful at running a business.

Now, the Church isn't there to fulfill every possible need. Just like many other companies, it now needs to work on "producing demand," that is, awakening needs where none exist. And it is certainly allowed to judge people's needs in the light of the Gospels. But it should always do so in respect and love, perceiving what people really require. Paul's Areopagus Sermon is a brilliant example of this. Wandering across the Areopagus, the Athenian market square, he sees many idols and is "deeply distressed" (Acts 17:16). But shortly thereafter, he has himself back under control: "Athenians, I see how extremely religious you are in every way. For as I went through the city and looked carefully at the objects of your worship, I found among them an altar with the inscription, 'To an unknown god.' What therefore you worship as unknown, this I proclaim to you" (Acts 17:22–23). At first it seems like a trick, this identification of an unknown God with the God of Jesus Christ. But what Paul is really doing is tapping into an unmet need among the Athenians—they are afraid of forgetting one of the many gods in heaven and have thus dedicated an altar to "the unknown god." By saying that, yes, this unknown god is the God of Jesus Christ, Paul is relieving the Athenians of their fear. They no longer need to feel terror of their unknown God. He loves mankind; he became man himself that we might see and witness him. Paul is making the Athenians a better offer.

If we proceed like this, we do not betray the gospel. The four evangelists themselves were masters of tailoring the testimony they received to the needs and context of their own congregation, as we certainly know today. We cannot and may not change the message, but we can alter how we transmit it. The missionary anger that seizes Paul briefly should not simply be dismissed either, for it helps him formulate his own position more clearly. But we as people of witness should never speak out of anger. That is devastating and not in line with the gospel.

The offer of faith also helps us. We should be in close contact with our own needs. If we repress our own truth and separate out our religiousness, our missionary work will not achieve anything in the long term. But if we let the Gospels give us what we need as well, we will be able to help others discover what they are missing, what they need. So, for example, if I have the need to pray, I should pray even if others can see it. Since I am starting out with my own incompleteness, my need, my weakness, I will not be "loud" or violent in my testimony. But at the same time, others can see how they, too, can have their needs met.

## OFFERING FREEDOM

Missionary work includes approaching and transcending boundaries and borders, be they social, linguistic, cultural, or national. But we must remember this: transcending our own borders—yes; transcending others' borders—no! We must respect this fundamental condition for missionary work.[5] Respect includes granting others unlimited freedom to be interested in the faith, to choose Christ—or to do precisely the opposite. Here, too, we must take Jesus as our yardstick. He never forced faith on others. The distorted image of missionaries "oppressing" or manipulating others into the faith has never been based on Jesus. It is theologically clear that faith is the free and independent choice in favor of God. And no one can make this choice for me. Imposed faith is no faith. God desires a free "yes" in response to his offer of Love. Even if I love someone, I cannot force them to love me—that is his or her freedom entirely. Love and freedom go hand in hand.

When a young man approaches Christ full of enthusiasm and devotion, ready to be sent by him ("Good Teacher, what must I do to inherit eternal life?" [Mark 10:17]), Jesus talks with him for some time and then encourages him to give his wealth to the poor. At that moment, however, the man is not yet capable of or willing to do so, and so Jesus lets him go without further comment and without any rebuke. He respects the man's "no" and even "loved him," as Mark 10:21 tells us.

Of course, it is upsetting when our offer of love is not reciprocated. And in this, too, we see Jesus open about his feelings, crying for those who reject him: "As he came near and saw the city, he wept over it, saying, 'If you, even you, had only recognized on this day the things that make for peace!'" (Luke 19:41–42). But Jesus still never uses force. On the contrary, he would rather suffer himself than do harm or injustice to someone else. Part of faith is that freedom: "For you were called to freedom, brothers and sisters" (Gal 5:13). That is why others' freedom may never be curtailed by our missionary work—though we may challenge it. The coming to faith is often felt as a "liberation," and all Judeo-Christian history is based on stories of liberation: freeing Israel from its slavery in Egypt. Jesus Christ, freeing people of sickness, of sin and death. Offering faith, therefore, also means offering freedom. In Jesus' case, his role model was likely his father, who never forced him to do anything either. When it transpired that Jesus was to sacrifice his life, he clearly articulated his fear and his inner resistance. This reflects the fact that Jesus experienced himself as a free person whose will was respected even by the almighty God-Father. When he finally agrees ("yet, not my will but yours be done" [Luke 22:42]), he accedes of his own free will. His self-sacrifice from love would have made no sense if it had been forced. God's history with his people has always been marked by nothing more than God's *attempts* to win back his people. He could never force them because he himself had given them freedom. He would have had to act against his own will, which he cannot do.

The history of Christian mission has always also been shaped by violence. People were pressured to convert, sometimes even given a false choice: "baptism or death." Charlemagne's wars were brutal, though he was criticized for them by the Church. And recall the injustices heaped on Jews in medieval cities or the missteps of the mission in Latin America. Here—in complete departure from the Gospels—mission was confused with power and right to rule. That casts the missionaries themselves, but not the gospel, in a very poor light.

As Christians, we must humbly acknowledge the sins of our ancestors and attempt never to repeat them. But we need not to let the populist prejudice of many of our contemporaries—that mission can be equated to violence—make us too shy to open our mouths. Pope Francis's views, expressed in his 2013 message for World Mission Day, are similar: "Sometimes, it is still thought that proclaiming the truth of the Gospel means an assault on freedom. Paul VI speaks eloquently on this: 'It would be…an error to impose something on the consciences of our brethren. But to propose to their consciences the truth of the Gospel and salvation in Jesus Christ, with complete clarity and with total respect for free options which it presents…is a tribute to this freedom' (*Evangelii Nuntiandi*, 80). We must always have the courage and the joy of proposing, with respect, an encounter with Christ, and being heralds of his Gospel."[6]

The large, Western organizations dedicated to mission, and particularly to mission in developing countries, all contribute to liberating, not oppressing, people. The Pontifical Mission Societies, or the Boniface Association and Renovabis in my native Germany, all speak out about injustice and violence and work against them, rather than use them.

## BEING COMPASSIONATE

Jesus empathized with people, he *felt with* them. When others suffer, their suffering enters his body as well. When he encountered a widow who had lost her only son, he "had compassion for her" (Luke 7:13). The literal wording of the original Gospel of Luke is this: "His innards turned over within his body."[7] Being of the same God-Father, he feels responsible and uses his closeness to the Father to help the suffering brother or suffering sister.

Today, active brotherly and sisterly love is the most eloquent witness we can bear. When we turn toward those to whom no one else will turn, we are giving testimony without ever even having to preach; we are imitating Jesus, who has proclaimed the God of loving-kindness. God's nature becomes visible and tangible through our actions.

In an interview with the Jesuit priest Antonio Spadaro, Pope Francis draws a picture of the Church as a "field hospital after a battle." He longs for a Church that primarily cares for people when they have been wounded by life, by others, or by themselves. "One must heal the wounds. Then we can speak of everything else." The word *compassion* is better here than *sympathy* because it prevents us from seeing the sufferer as an object. Many people don't want sympathy. Compassion, however, treats the sufferer as the subject.[8] It is also greater than empathy, which often stays just a feeling. Compassion includes this emotion, but goes beyond it into a kind of attitude, an approach, the mindset of loving-kindness directed toward the sufferer. This makes clear that it is a kind of activity in solidarity with the sufferer, taking his side and together trying to limit suffering or to resolve it.

A healthy missionary approach seeks to let people feel the good news, not just proclaim it. For example, in Tanzania, missionary Benedictines have dug wells, built hospitals, erected schoolhouses. The Verbum Dei sisters go to the poor. There are countless Christians all over the world who, in ways large and small, help reduce the suffering of the poor. Christians are most needed wherever there is suffering or poverty. Our saturated, safe society can sometimes make it difficult to identify the "poor"—for one thing, we tend to avert our eyes. But there is also a great deal of "hidden poverty." I remember how, working as an educator in our monastery boarding school, I would notice that often children, particularly from very rich families, were decrepit of soul. It was painful to see how, despite their material wealth, they were somehow poor in their relationships, alone in their hearts. At the time, we called it "the poverty of wealth."

That makes it important for us to ask, What are people hungering for? This means looking less for situations in which we can proclaim the gospel and more for this kind of hunger. It is where Jesus would go today. Jesus' compassion even went so far that he shared the lot of the outcast and was executed on the cross, like a criminal. In dying, he let out a scream. The Son of God, here in an hour of utmost need, himself cries out to God. It is also the moment in which—almost as a byproduct—conversion occurs: a nonbeliever, a Roman captain, is so moved by what he experiences that he confesses his faith in Jesus: "Truly this man was God's Son!" (Mark 15:39).[9]

## AWAITING CHRIST

As noted earlier, in the past, there was an extremely strong "drive" for missionary activities: the goal was saving souls. The Church's claim of absoluteness—*extra ecclesia nulla salus*, or "no salvation outside the Church"—implied that mission was a matter of life or death. It was an all-in proposition, not just a question of this life but of whether a person would know eternal love, joy, freedom, and salvation in God or not. It was understood that anyone who was not baptized could never find these. The missionary energy of this time was like that of firefighters. They know that the house is burning and that, if they do not save them, no one will. That is how we can explain the almost infinite self-sacrifice of early missionaries. They were willing to sacrifice anything because the stakes were infinitely high. This gave their lives a deep sense of fulfillment and meaning, just as a firefighter is fulfilled by the lives that he saves.

The Second Vatican Council did not drop the Church's claim of absolute truth, but it has embedded it in a larger perspective, as we will explore below. The Church is convinced that a person who, in principle, is open to transcendental experience can be saved. In every person, there is a divine core that cannot be given or taken away. There is a final hope for every human being. Unfortunately, this final hope—the revelation of which should be embraced—has led to complacency and a widespread abandonment of missionary activity. To continue the metaphor of firefighting: Why should I run into a burning house if I know that everyone in it will survive anyway?

How can we feel an urgency in bearing witness today, an urgency that is fed by far more than just the fear that in the future, all our churches will stand empty or be converted to museums? There is a further theological motif worth noting here that may have lost some of its popularity but none of its aptness. That image is the so-called Second Coming. The New Testament describes Christians as awaiting Christ's return in the imminent future. This "Second Coming of Christ" was interpreted as the completion of the kingdom of God but also as the Day of Judgment. The Apostle Paul was one missionary who lived fully in this conviction. For example, he considered it less important whether one was married or unmarried, as the Second Coming would wash away such categories (see 1 Cor 7:26-27). For early Christians, this had two results: first, it brought a great anticipatory joy, since all suffering and injustice would be ended; and second, it encouraged spiritual work, since one wanted to be well prepared for when God returned.

The dynamism of the spread of Christianity can only truly be explained by the expectation of an imminent Second Coming. When Christ's return was not immediate, however, the Church was established as a lasting institution. The conviction of Christ's return was not abandoned and is alive even today, but its liveliness has dimmed.

Missionaries are people who focus particularly on this aspect of their faith. They are "running" (see Gal 2:2) rather than walking because their work is so important.[10] Peter is particularly clear on this point:

> But do not ignore this one fact, beloved, that with the Lord one day is like a thousand years, and a thousand years are like one day. The Lord is not slow about his promise, as some think of slowness, but is patient with you, not wanting any to perish, but all to come to repentance. But the day of the Lord will come like a thief, and then the heavens will pass away with a loud noise, and the elements will be dissolved with fire, and the earth and everything that is done on it will be disclosed.
>
> Since all these things are to be dissolved in this way, what sort of persons ought you to be in leading lives of holiness and godliness, waiting for and hastening the coming of the day of God, because of which the heavens will be set ablaze and dissolved, and the elements will melt with fire? But, in accordance with his promise, we wait for new heavens and a new earth, where righteousness is at home. (2 Peter 3:8-13)

What a remarkable thought, that we can "accelerate" the return of the Lord! Naturally, it is Christ's decision when he returns and when a new heaven and earth can be vouchsafed us by God. Nevertheless, if we are vines in the vineyard, if the

Church is the Body of Christ, then we do have some influence on this Second Coming. As soon as we start living today as our faith has longed for, the kingdom of God is realized more quickly. God does not want to wait anymore! He does so because he is patient. He does so because he respects our freedom. And we still behave as though nothing had happened! As missionaries, we go before the Lord wherever he wants to go, until in the end—with our help, as well—he will have gone everywhere. Benedict's *Rule* closes with this: "Christ himself, and may he bring us all together to eternal life."[11] The idea that we can only enter heaven *all together* has something that both incites and reassures us. No one is left behind. But whatever else may be the case, we should begin with ourselves, from a place of spiritual renewal, living according to the measures of the kingdom of God. The more people we take with us, the faster we personally reach our goal.

Monks have a special relationship with this kind of goal, as well. Recalling the parable of the servant whom the returning lord finds awake and waiting, they consider themselves "the wakeful ones." Therefore, the monks' characteristic prayer is the Vigil, originally prayed in the middle of the night. Though the Book of Hours no longer knows such a time for prayer, the monks in some cases still arise and are wakeful in the middle of the night—or at least very early in the morning—to pray. By doing so, they are keeping attuned to the reality that the Lord will return—and can return at any moment.

But wakefulness is demanded of both the missionary and the monk alike during the day, as well. Has the Lord perhaps returned already? Where does he reveal himself at this very moment? Where is he in those whom I encounter? Instead of consuming substances or ideas that dull the senses, the monk and missionary want to be particularly sober and wakeful. They want to have "their wits about them"—to be in oneself, not out-side oneself—in order to welcome the Lord.

The Swiss Benedictine nun Silja Walter (1919–2011) sang of this truth in a poem: "Someone must be home, Lord, when You come." Perhaps Christ is trying to come, but we simply aren't home. The monks want to be at home when the Lord comes, which is why they have taken a vow of "stability" to be at the place of their monastery forever.

Jesus teaches his disciples about his return. He compares it to a thief who steals into the house when no one is expecting it (see Matt 24:43–44). That is why monks must "preserve their salinity," as it were (see Matt 5:13). A missionary who has become shallow can neither have a positive influence on the world and the people around him nor be willing to embody God's unpredictable arrival.

For this reason, the basic missionary attitude is one of mindfulness, wakefulness, and attention. As Benedict writes in the prologue of his *Rule*: "However late, then, it may seem, let us rouse ourselves from lethargy. That is what scripture urges on us when it says: The time has come to rouse ourselves from sleep. Let us open our eyes to the light that can change us into the likeness of God. Let our ears be alert to the stirring call of his voice crying to us every day: Today, if you should hear this voice, do not harden your hearts."[12] In other words, expecting the Lord daily with all our senses, just as one might expect the arrival of a dear friend.

The Germans say that "the greatest joy is in anticipation." Do you know that feeling of standing at a train station or air-port and waiting for the arrival of a dear friend? What a sense of excitement, of butterflies in the stomach! This same feeling is evoked in the Gospel of Luke: Mary, pregnant with Jesus, goes to visit her likewise pregnant cousin, Elizabeth, and the women's joy is multiplied by their companionship. "When Elizabeth heard Mary's greeting, the child leaped in her womb" (Luke 1:41). When we prepare the way of the Lord, helping him be born in and among the people, we are taking on the role of Mary and Elizabeth. What a joy to feel the anticipation of his coming! What a joy to be present at the moment that new life enters the world!

Missionaries are people of good hope. They spread hope because there is something left to expect. Life is not just a flash in the pan, a rat race, or a self-service station. There is something coming; there is someone coming. Even after death, you still have a future, and the world still has a future, even after its death. Missionaries are people who hold their head high. "Now when these things begin to take place, stand up and raise your heads, because your redemption is drawing near" (Luke 21:28).

## A GLOBAL COMMUNITY

One of the main characteristics of missionary work is going beyond your own borders. As noted earlier, this might consist simply of going outside and encountering my neighbor. We are right to notice that, in recent years, Germany and the West have somehow become "missionary countries." That means that we don't need to go for a long drive to get started. However, international and global perspectives have always been and continue to be an important aspect of the missionary project. While it's dangerous to describe all that we do in our own surroundings as "missionary work," we also shouldn't define mission too narrowly; the classic "*missio ad extra*," or outward mission, which traverses continents, continues to be important, maybe more so than ever.

There are several reasons for this. For one thing, the Church has the advantage of already being global, whereas the world at large is still busy working toward a meaning or purpose for globalization—as exemplified by the Pope's *Urbi et Orbi* blessing for the entire world. When youths of all countries travel to the Church's World Youth Day, what they remember is the internationality and variety of cultures. Meanwhile, programs where youths can become "temporary missionaries" are more popular than ever, and many orders and dioceses offer such options, both in Europe and in North America. Young people are recognizing that to move appropriately in the world, they need to be open to the concerns, problems, advantages, and peculiarities of other countries and cultures. For those who want to go abroad, at least a brief period, the church has an invaluable network of dioceses and parishes, communities and monasteries.

The Church has traditionally seen itself as a local church, and in a community and on the ground, it is a "Church" in the full sense of the word. Nothing is missing. The bishop is the first shepherd. But from its beginnings, churches have always found it necessary to look past their own borders and cultivate a lively exchange with other local churches. By doing so, they guard themselves against provincialism. Learning from the churches of other countries and continents offers a wonderful opportunity. After all, the Holy Spirit is at work there as well.

For example, the German church is often caught up in structural questions. But these concerns seem less vital when we look at the immediate vitality of the Church in other countries. Sure, our German situation is a special one, based on all the concordats and our history, and in that situation, we need to find our own way. But Germany is also the one country in the world to pay an official church tax, and it nevertheless has much to learn from other countries about what it means as an active Christian to make financial sacrifices for a common goal. That

process can strengthen the identification that is so often missing in Germany.

Looking beyond our borders is part of the mission of
today. Since faith is always transcendent and crosses boundaries, every Christian's missionary approach is made manifest in
their willingness to learn from other countries and cultures
while not considering one's own lifestyle the gold standard.
Internationality and global consciousness have been part of the
Christian identity from the very beginning—the Church arose on
Pentecost, in one multilingual instant.

The various missionary aid organizations, the missionaries
and lay volunteers with international activities, the youth in
their exchange programs—all of them are invited to talk about
the political, cultural, and spiritual situation in other countries.
Missionaries are communicators first, everything else second:
they tell people how Christian life is implemented in other parts
of the world. The full power of this missionary idea can only be
realized once we transcend national, cultural, and linguistic
barriers. The flipside is that, when we expose ourselves to other
countries and cultures, it is easier for us to respect the differences of religion, culture, lifestyle, or opinion we find at home.
When I am in a foreign country, I am automatically more wakeful and attentive. But when I see my neighbors, the first things
that come to mind are my own prejudices, and I cannot see with
the eyes of Jesus, who sees my neighbors new and in the light of
love every day.

The words of my local pastor, who was born in the Congo,
show how varied and fruitful international exchange can be:

> "Until now I didn't really see myself as a missionary in
> the typical sense. I see a typical missionary as a
> priest—or brother in an order, or a sister in an order,
> or a layperson—who feels a calling to do pastoral

work in a place other than his home region and is then sent (Latin: *missus*) there. For myself, I came to Germany in 1996 to get my doctorate in theology here and then return to my home country, the Democratic Republic of Congo. But my "short" planned stay for studying turned into a full seventeen years with real pastoral duties in Germany. Those duties outside my own country of the Congo mean that one could certainly view me as a missionary. The Church is always missionary—meaning sent to people—to be a sign amid our world of the impending kingdom of God in our time."

Here we can see an international understanding of mission.

## INTERRELIGIOUS DIALOGUE

The monastic orders have long had close relationships with other religions.[13] This may be because monks are especially suited for beginning such dialogue with other religions, as they are able to encounter the monks of other religions and other orders and speak about their experiences. This religious exchange is always respectful and friendly; there is never an argument. Monasticism is a phenomenon that crosses religious boundaries: Buddhism and Christianity have the longest traditions, and Sufi Islam is an attempt to reactivate a Muslim monastic tradition. The shared spiritual elements of silence, fasting, meditation, reading, singing, communal life, and discipline form a good basis for exchanging experiences and views.

The people, however, who have experience with such dialogue recognize that religions are quite different and that they can't be "put in a box" together. The central connecting element may be the "mystery" that each tradition claims. The doors for interreligious dialogue about differences and similarities, however, have been opened ever since the Second Vatican Council. This dialogue is a natural fruit of what "mission" is in its innermost essence: If mission means to transcend borders, then we are encountering not only foreign countries and cultures but also other religions. This encounter is where exchange happens, and in that exchange, we can learn from one another. Pope John Paul II, one of the most missionary popes of our time, traveled to many countries and instigated the first World Day of Prayer for Peace in Assisi, during which clergy and believers of various religions meet for dialogue and prayer. He writes, "My contact with representatives of the non-Christian spiritual traditions, particularly those of Asia, has confirmed me in the view that the future of mission depends to a great extent on contemplation. Unless the missionary is a contemplative he cannot proclaim Christ in a credible way. He is a witness to the experience of God, and must be able to say with the apostles: 'that which we have looked upon...concerning the word of life...we proclaim also to you' (1 John 1:1-3)."[14] What we read here is a beautiful example of how even the pope can learn from other religions.

Interreligious dialogue does more to advance each individual religion than isolation ever could. Or, as the Islamic philosopher Abu Hamid Muhammad bin Muhammad al-Ghazāli noted, "The harm inflicted on religion by those who defend it in a way not proper to it is greater than the harm inflicted upon religion by those who attack it in a way proper to it."[15] Those who truly trust their God need not fear that another's religion may be true.

In a way, each religion makes its own claim of absoluteness, believing itself not only to be true, but rather, to be the last and insuperable truth. Each religion believes that all people, no matter of what creed, will, in the end, be revealed as connected to its own God. If that is indeed the case, then one can let all religions touch one's life: the hidden God who has made all things will then connect us.

Nevertheless, encountering other religions does not mean we should be aiming for some sort of "super-religion" in which everything fits together. Nor does it mean that we get to pick and choose those aspects of each religion that we happen to like at that moment. An interreligious dialogue presupposes and necessitates high-profile, established, and subtle partners for said dialogue. The longer I walk the path of Christianity, the more I realize that it tends to demand "more" of me rather than less. It calls me to greater consistency, deeper understanding— and any kind of simple syncretism gets in the way of that. The Dalai Lama himself recommends that everyone stay in his or her own tradition and grow within it. In theory, there may be many commonalities, but practice is hermetic.

Consequently, Christian mission today is all but unthinkable without a conversation between the religions. That dialogue won't mean we lose our own identity; it will help us discover it.

## BEING PRESENT

Understanding mission as an offer connects us to another paradigm: "Mission as Presence." Presence means even more than offer or gift because it involves upholding the offer, keeping it available. I can well remember how the sisters of a Protestant monastic community shared their missionary experience with me. After the fall of the Berlin Wall, the Communität Casteller Ring, a monastic order, had quickly founded a branch of their society in the former East German Erfurt, in precisely the same cloister where Martin Luther had lost his appetite for monastic life. People from the surrounding area accepted this courage with admiration and love. The sisters told me, "The people here like us a great deal. They tell us, so many people came from West Germany after the wall fell—banks, stores, and churches, too. But, after a while, so many left. But you're still here!" The pure presence and stability of these sisters were admired and were a way of bearing witness. People wondered, What's different about these sisters? It appears they don't just want our money like all the other people who came after reunification. Merely the presence and stability of these sisters sent positive ripples through the largely atheist population of the town. It is sad that the order was unable to keep the cloister open due to lack of personnel.

At the conference, "Mission and Monasticism," in Rome in 2009,[16] the question was raised of what mission would need to look like in an Islamic country, where Christian mission is generally forbidden by law. If *activities*, such as praying and advertising, are forbidden, one can still bear witness through one's presence. The silence of monks can be heard loud and clear without their ever having to say a word. In fact, not too long ago, this idea became a terrifying reality. Back in 1938, French monks had gone to Tibhirine in Algeria to pray and work. They had no missionary intentions but simply wanted to practice their monastic calling in peace. One of their characteristics—as with all monks—was hospitality, and so they cherished contact with local people, all of whom were of the Muslim faith. The monks tried to learn the language, studied the Qur'an, and offered medical assistance in order to serve their community and maintain friendly relations with their neighbors. But, in the confusion of the Civil Wars in the 1990s, they, too, became subject to persecution, even though they took no political position. In the end, they were taken hostage and murdered. This was in 1996. Only two monks survived.[17] Their presence alone radiated enough power to make them so threatening. They did not even have to do anything. That they were simply *present* was enough.

In an increasingly secularized society, remaining a Christian is already an act of witness and can at times be provocative. This means we shouldn't be frustrated if, when talking about our faith, we don't arrive at the point where people want to listen to us. But continuing on and not letting ourselves be dissuaded—always remaining open and yet firm—is our service for the people to whom we speak. That is what Christ has tasked us to do. And doing so has a quiet but enormous power in such a rapidly changing world. Being a Christian and living as one is already the expression of a missionary frame of mind. Conversely, those people who simply want to live peacefully as Christians—the Tibhirine monks, for example—are practically urged to bear witness by the dynamics of the world around them. The Tibhirine monks never wanted to be missionaries, much less martyrs. It was their presence that made them thus. It was certainly not their first choice to go to the death for Christ. It was a consequence of their presence. All they wanted to do was stay; and yet they had to go, just like Jesus himself. But that has only made their testimony that much more powerful. Incidentally, the Muslim faithful near the monastery had urged the monks to stay. They were good friends to the monks. Once, they even confessed the following metaphor: "You are the tree, and we are the birds perching on it."

# CONCLUSION

Jesus' call to mission, which closes the Gospel of Matthew, ends with these words: "And remember, I am with you always, to the end of the age" (Matt 28:20). Let's consider these words. At the end of the world, the end of the age—the outermost places we can go in spatial, temporal, social, psychic dimensions—there everywhere is Christ with us. And we may go there without fear precisely because he is already there. Our gift is that we can make his love visible to the people.

## ABSOLUTENESS

In the Middle Ages, the German mystic Meister Eckhart (ca. 1260–1327) developed a theology and spirituality that is particularly current today, seven hundred years later. His thinking revolves around God as center. There is nothing outside God, and only if we have let go all dependence on earthly things, will we be in the place where there is nothing else than God and be one with God.[1] Taken at face value, this is an insuperable claim to absoluteness: there is no salvation outside God. But one could also call it a claim to "absoluteness in release." Only when I have released—let go of—everything, *even God*, will I be on the side of the absolute.

The question is how to conceptualize the claim of absoluteness today. There can be no religion without a claim to absoluteness. If God, then God! But people have had too many bad experiences with religion, so they are afraid of religions and this demand for absoluteness. Particularly the monotheistic religions of Judaism, Christianity, and Islam are suspected of using this standard of absoluteness to perpetuate a strategy of conquest. The practice of the Christian Church in the last decades has been such that it need no longer countenance this reproach. And the theory, too, has changed somewhat.[2]

Reflecting on the term *absolute* can help. *Absolute* literally means "detached, not connected, released" (from the Latin *absolvere*, "to release or separate off"). In other words, by invoking absoluteness is that God exists regardless, unconnected to the world, whether we want him to or not and whether we believe or not. He is not "contingent," that is, dependent on our thought. He is the absolute truth on which we have only limited, conditional influence.

Each religion now bears the risk of individual believers, groups, churches, or even the Church trying to make God their "property," so to speak. This attitude is summed up by the German songwriter Herbert Grönemeyer, who wrote the lyric, *"Mit Gott auf unserer Seite, mit Jesus in einem Boot"*—"With God on our side, in the same boat as Jesus." But people who claim this kind of relationship with God cannot refer to the origins of the Christian faith. God's kingdom has been realized in the Church in a very special way because God has chosen the Church and made a covenant with it. But the Church is not identical to the kingdom of God that Jesus founded and that the Holy Spirit continues to build among us. The Church and the individual will always lag behind that standard. They have their tendency to sin, that is, to turn away from the living God. They are dependent on God's forgiveness. The crucial point is that they are not God but are limited.

But, if we follow God's absoluteness to its logical conclusion, we can face the danger of trying to "possess" God. Any claim to absoluteness that relies on shutting out others cannot be whole. God is not one thing or another, but he also isn't *not* the one thing or the other. This claim to absoluteness is exclusive by being *radically inclusive*. It is so inclusive that it includes and respects even human freedom. What results in practice is the release we noted earlier, in the knowledge and faith that we are on the right path while being free to turning back continuously to God anew. This freedom points to God's transcendence. It is atheism that in the end discovered just this concept and developed "Atheism 2.0," represented particularly by Alain de Botton in the United Kingdom. This atheism sees itself as so absolute that it can afford to include everything. This means that even religious structures are no longer categorically excluded, to relinquish the denial-based dependence of A-Theism. Religions are acceptable if the people who engage in them find them so. A little Christianity here, a little Buddhism there—and why not? But the difference remains: Atheism 2.0 is still dependent, only on itself, on people. But Christian religion wants to be radically absolute and releasing. We have a choice: Would we rather be dependent on ourselves or on God? I, personally, prefer God, because I know myself and my limitations, as well as those of my fellow man. But any person who professes to be completely "independent" is denying his own limitations. This makes him proud and, in a certain way, he is making himself into a god.

## ALL-ENCOMPASSING

One could also take the word *catholic* as a starting point for explaining the claim to absoluteness. Here I don't mean *Catholic* in the confessional sense it has had since the sixteenth century, but in the sense used long before the schism, as in the creed of AD 381. The Greek word *katholos* means "all-encompassing."

This includes that same claim to absoluteness. Translated into a missionary dimension, it means that the further we go, the more catholic we must become. Narrowness and exclusivity, which are born of fear, are not signs of a healthy Christianity or Catholicism.

The Psalmist proclaims, "Your steadfast love, O LORD, extends to the heavens, / your faithfulness to the clouds" (Ps 36:5); "Your name, O God, like your praise, / reaches to the ends of the earth. / Your right hand is filled with victory" (Ps 48:10). The Christian claim to absoluteness goes beyond the philosophical dimension. It has a face. As Jesus says of himself in the Gospel of John, "I am the way, and the truth, and the life" (14:6). God's absolute truth becomes visible in a specific face, becomes audible in a specific voice. This "dependence" thus happens eye-to-eye, on one level with one another. It has become comprehensible and tangible. God is so radically all-encompassing and inclusive that in a natural way, with joy and ease, God includes humanity in his absoluteness through his Son, Jesus the Man.

The one holy day that most clearly illustrates the idea of "absoluteness in release" is the Feast of the Epiphany. On January 6, the Church celebrates the fact that the entire world—represented by the Three Kings, or Wise Men, from various parts of the earth—comes to the manger to pay homage to Jesus. What is encouraging about this event? First, the Absolute is not only human, but in fact a baby! There is no more sympathetic way to cast the claim of absoluteness. Second, those accepting the absolute child are kings or wise men. They are rulers, people of high name and stature, the most educated of their time, the people whom others ought to respect. Accepting the absolute does not decrease our human dignity; quite the contrary! In other words, God, the absolute, does not need to make men small for men to recognize him. And, finally, Christ's claim to absoluteness develops. None of the Three Wise Men are forced to visit the manger. Each chooses to follow the star that leads him to Christ. It is a path, one that requires time. It's *allowed* to require time. God has that time, and we need that time.

God does not need recognition. But it does us good to recognize God because it brings us in contact with the absolute, but also with the entire world—we meet the other Wise Men at the manger—and not least with our inner selves. We understand where our human dignity originates. Recognizing the greater truth can show us who we are and what we are called to do. The Wise Men return to their own kingdoms. We can also interpret the Feast of the Epiphany as illustrating that it is and will be Christ who will unite everybody, all people, all nations, all kingdoms. The United Nations, founded in 1948 after witnessing the destruction of which humanity is capable if unchecked, will not really be able to fulfill this promise, because people always have and always must have diverging interests. But the Christian religion can. In fact, it can thus make an immeasurable contribution to peaceful coexistence in the entire world—all through the concept of absoluteness.

When we kneel before the one unalterable truth, which is also the truth of the other, then we can let each other be in all our differences. The Three Wise Men do not quarrel at the side of the manger. And each of them returns to his kingdom. The Christian claim to absoluteness does not want to separate out anybody. It wants to unite everybody, just like Jesus wants to gather us all: "Jerusalem, Jerusalem," he says, "the city that kills the prophets and stones those who are sent to it! How often have I desired to gather your children together as a hen gathers her brood under her wings, and you were not willing!" (Luke 13:34).

If we want to go out, to go toward him on whom we all depend in equal measure because he gave us the gift of life, we all will be able to live together in peace. On the one hand, I cannot imagine how atheists might create a world in which everyone would live in peace and respect one another, because people have interests, and these interests must—at least temporarily—be mutually exclusive. For God, on the other hand, it is simpler to gather and unite us all. But for us to come to this point, we must leave our "comfort zones." All of us are strangers when we stand at the manger. And in this foreignness, we find Christ. That is why the missionary dimension is essential to the salvation of Christians and of the entire world.

Every person has something missionary within them— some more, some less. Each of us wants to make this world better. At certain points in our life, we feel the call to act in certain ways or to respond to certain convictions. This call has something imperative. Only if we follow it can our life have meaning—even if our mission consists of never proselytizing and convincing others of the importance of this stance. In that sense, there are billions of missionaries all over the world. Often, it is atheists who feel their own mission strongly. The unique opportunity of the Christian claim to absoluteness is that it humanizes this missionary aspect of our nature. By cultivating, placing it within a tradition, and in no small measure, limiting it, Christian absoluteness can humanize the innate will to improve the world, the desire to convince others of our own discovered deep insights. The Church's tradition and theology can help find the right scope for this project.

Cardinal Timothy Dolan of New York, on being created a Cardinal by Pope Benedict XVI, expressed his vision of the Church and its missionary practice as "confident yes, triumphant never!" I agree: proclaiming our faith confidently, with a good measure of self-assurance, but simultaneously without any hyperbole or feelings of superiority. In the end, I will kneel before the manger with the others, and the true King will be a child. If we look at our claim to absoluteness so gently and with such release of worldly concerns, we can become the kinds of Christians described in the Epistle of Mathetes to Diognetus (AD 2/3): "In a word, what the soul is in a body, this the Christians are in the world. The soul is spread through all the members of the body, and Christians through the diverse cities of the world. The soul hath its abode in the body, and yet it is not of the body. So Christians have their abode in the world, and yet they are not of the world" (Diognetus 6:1–3).[3]

## WE CANNOT BE SILENT

Shortly after the experience of Pentecost, the apostles Peter and John healed a lame man in the temple and spoke freely to the people about Jesus. The priests and scribes then called the two before the High Council "and ordered them not to speak or teach at all in the name of Jesus. But Peter and John answered them, 'Whether it is right in God's sight to listen to you rather than to God, you must judge; for we cannot keep from speaking about what we have seen and heard'" (Acts 4:18–20).

The Word that comes down to us through the apostles is unstoppable. I wish for all of us that we, too, become open to this Word. Once we have heard it, it is impossible to remain silent.

# NOTES

## INTRODUCTION: AN ABUNDANT HEART

1. Taken from one of the "interventions" to the College of Cardinals in the days that preceded the papal conclave and election of Cardinal Jorge Mario Bergoglio to the See of Peter in March 2013, the then-Archbishop of Buenos Aires gave a brief yet riveting talk on "The Sweet and Comforting Joy of Evangelizing."

2. Christopher Lasch, *The Culture of Narcissism: American Life in an Age of Diminishing Expectations* (New York: Warner Books, 1980).

## 1. BON VOYAGE!

1. See Wolfgang Günther, "Gott selbst treibt Mission: Das Modell der '*Missio Dei*,'" in *Plädoyer für Mission: Beiträge zum Verständnis von Mission heute*, ed. Klaus Schäfer (Hamburg: Evangelisches Missionswerk in Deutschland, 1998).

## 2. BEFORE SETTING OUT

1. See St. Benedict, *RB 1980: The Rule of St. Benedict*, trans. and ed. Timothy Fry, Timothy Horner, and Imogene Baker (Collegeville, MN: Liturgical Press, 1982).

2. Naomi L. Quenk, *Essentials of Myers-Briggs Type Indicator Assessment* (New York: John Wiley & Sons, 2008).

3. See Susan Cain, *Quiet: The Power of Introverts in a World that Can't Stop Talking* (New York: Crown Publishing, 2012).

# 3. UNDERSTANDING "MISSION"

1. Conference of Superiors of Missionary Orders in Germany, *Von der alten Mission zur neuen Evangelisierung* [From old Mission to New Evangelization], Nuremberg: Deutsche Ordensoberkonferenz, 2013.

2. Translator's note: "Strength through Joy" (*Kraft durch Freude*) was the name of a leisure organization run by Germany's National Socialist government under Hitler.

3. The declaration is available online at http://www.vatican .va/archive/hist_councils/ii_vatican_council/documents/vat-ii_decl _19651028_nostra-aetate_en.html (accessed October 3, 2018).

4. "Zeit der Aussaat: Missionarisch Kirche sein," cited in Georg Augustin and Klaus Krämer, eds., *Mission als Herausforderung: Impulse zur Neuevangelisierung* [Mission as Challenge: Impulses for New Evangelization] (Freiburg: Herder, 2011).

5. See also my previous book *Ich verstehe Dich nicht. Die Herzensreise des Kleinen Prinzen* [I Don't Understand You: The Little Prince's Journey of the Heart], 4th ed. (Münsterschwarzach: Vier-Türme-Verlag, 2004).

6. "We are called on 'to go anywhere across the geographical and cultural frontiers where there is need of working with Christ.'" See https://jesuits.org/aboutus?PAGE=DTN-20130520123826 (accessed October 3, 2018).

7. See Gal 2; Acts 15.

8. See Willy Manzanza, *Gedanken eines Importpriesters* [Thoughts of an Imported Priest ] (Hildesheim: Moritzberg Verlag, 2013).

9. From a 2012 lecture before the general chapter of Missionary Benedictines in Damme: Julia D. E. Prinz, VDMF, *Gratitude, Hunger, and Apocalyptic: A Missionary Existence in the Spirit of Verbum Dei*.

10. Louis J. Luzbetak, *The Church and Cultures: New Perspectives in Missiological Anthropology* (New York: Orbis Books, 1988).

11. *Omnia videre, multa dissimulare, pauca corrigere.*

12. St. Benedict, *Saint Benedict's Rule*, trans. Patrick Barry (Mahwah, NJ: HiddenSpring), 55.

13. Ansgar Stüfe and Fidelis Ruppert, *Der Abt als Arzt—der Arzt als Abt: Anregungen aus der Benediktsregel* [The Abbot as Doctor—the Doctor as Abbot: Suggestions from Benedict's Rule] (Münsterschwarzach: Vier Türme, 1997).

14. Nikolaus Nonn, *Willkommen! Vom Segen der Gastfreundschaft* [Welcome! On the blessing of hospitality] (Münsterschwarzach: Vier Türme, 2011).

15. Bede, *Historia ecclesiastica gentes Anglorum*, ed. B. Colgrave and R. A. B. Mynors (Oxford: Oxford University Press. 1969), I c. 26, 76–77. Translated by the author.

16. Conrad Leyser, "Gregory the Great and Gregorian Tradition: Memory, Contemplation, and the Missionary Frontier," in *Mission and Monasticism: Acts of the International Symposium at the Pontifical Athenaeum S. Anselmo, Rome, May 7–9, 2009,* ed. Conrad Leyser and Hannah Williams (St. Ottilien: EOS, 2013), 47–53.

17. See Anton Scharer, "Insular Mission to the Continent in the Early Middle Ages," in Leyser and Williams, eds., *Mission and Monasticism,* 56–62. Other significant missionary monks besides Augustine of Canterbury and Aidan of Lindisfarne include St. Columbanus (590), who missionized around Lake Constance; Willibrord (658–739), who went to today's Netherlands as a missionary; and Wilfrid (634–709), who missionized to the Frisians and Thuringians, founding Echternach Abbey.

18. Jonathan Düring, *Ihr seid das Salz, nicht die Suppe. Von der befreienden Kraft des frohen Glaubens* [You are the Salt, not the Soup: The liberating power of joyful faith] (Münsterschwarzach: Vier Türme, 2009).

19. See Gregory the Great, *Der hl. Benedikt* [St. Benedict] (St. Ottilien: EOS, 1995), 193.

20. See Gregory the Great, *Der hl. Benedikt,* 183.

21. This idea was developed by the Benedictine professor Jeremy Driscoll in a lecture to U.S. Benedictine abbots held in February 2014, in Cullman, Alabama. The workshop explored the question of how monks can contribute to re-evangelization.

# 4. BEARING WITNESS

1. See Mauritius Wilde, *Peter und Paulus: Wer in Gruppen entscheidet* [Peter and Paul: Who makes decisions in groups] (Münsterschwarzach: Vier Türme, 2003).

2. Meister Eckhart, "Sermon 109 (26)," in *Deutsche Predigten und Traktate* [German sermons and tracts], ed. J. Quint (Zürich: Diogenes Verlag, 1979).

3. St. Augustine. *Confessions.* Translated from the original Latin by the author.

4. Regina Nothelle and Sabine Zarden, "Dialogpredigt vom Weltmissionssonntag 2013 in der Propsteigemeinde St. Trinitatis, Leipzig" [Dialogue sermon on world mission day in the Leipzig Propstei Parish of the Holy Trinity], October 27, 2013. The complete sermon (in German) may be read at http://www.orientierung-leipzig .de/kontaktstelle/predigten/23-predigten/343-wir-sind-fuer-mission (accessed October 5, 2018).

# 6. OUR RELATIONSHIP WITH THE CHURCH

1. Accessible online at https://w2.vatican.va/content/francesco/ en/messages/missions/documents/papa-francesco_20130519 _giornata-missionaria2013.html (accessed September 7, 2017).

2. St. Benedict, *Saint Benedict's Rule,* trans. Patrick Barry (Mahwah, NJ: HiddenSpring), 117.

3. *St. Benedict's Rule*, 151.

# 7. RETURNING HOME TO CHRIST

1. Archbishop Timothy Dolan's Address to Pope Benedict XVI upon being created a Cardinal, Rome, February 17, 2012. See full text at https://cnsblog.wordpress.com/2012/02/17/cardinal-designate -dolans-address-to-pope-benedict-and-the-college-of-cardinals/ (accessed July 12, 2018).

2. Johannes Mahr, *Die Märtyrer von Tokwon: Glaubenszeugen in Korea 1950–1952* [The martyrs of Tokwon: Witnessbearers in Korea, 1950–1952] (St. Ottilien: EOS Editions, 2011).

3. Available in English online at http://w2.vatican.va/content/john-paul-ii/en/encyclicals/documents/hf_jp-ii_enc_07121990_redemptoris-missio.html (accessed October 9, 2018).

# 8. THE FUNDAMENTALS OF BEING A MISSIONARY

1. See, for example, Stephen B. Bevans and Roger P. Schroeder, *Constants in Context: A Theology of Mission for Today* (New York: Orbis Books, 2004).

2. John Paul II, Speech to the Assembly of CELAM, Port-au-Prince, Haiti, 1983. Available through the Vatican website in Italian, Spanish, and Portuguese at https://w2.vatican.va/content/john-paul-ii/it/speeches/1983/march/documents/hf_jp-ii_spe_19830309_assemblea-celam.html (accessed October 9, 2018). Excerpt translated from Spanish by P. Dahm Robertson.

3. St. Benedict, *Saint Benedict's Rule,* trans. Patrick Barry (Mahwah, NJ: HiddenSpring), 45.

4. Second Vatican Council, *Gaudium et Spes: Pastoral Constitution in the Modern World*, December 7, 1965. Available online at http://www.vatican.va/archive/hist_councils/ii_vatican_council/documents/vat-ii_const_19651207_gaudium-et-spes_en.html.

5. See Mauritius Wilde, *Respekt. Die Kunst der gegenseitigen Wertschätzung* [Respect: The Art of Mutual Appreciation] (Münsterschwarzach: Vier Türme, 2009).

6. Pope Francis, "Message of Pope Francis for World Mission Day," no. 3. Available online at https://w2.vatican.va/content/francesco/en/messages/missions/documents/papa-francesco_20130519_giornata-missionaria2013.html.

7. François Bovon, *Das Evangelium nach Lukas*, in EKK (Evangelisch-katholischer Kommentar zum Neuen Testament), vol. III/1 (Benziger Verlag, Zürich, 1989), 362.

8. See Lothar Kuld, *Compassion. Raus aus der Ego-Falle* [Compassion: Escaping the Ego Trap] (Münsterschwarzach: Vier Türme, 2003).

9. See the following lecture held at the 2012 general chapter of missionary Benedictines in Damme: Julia D. E. Prinz, VDMF, "Gratitude, Hunger and Apocalyptic: A Missionary Existence in the Spirit of Dei Verbum." See also Julia D. E. Prinz, *Endangering Hunger for God: Johann Baptist Metz and Dorothee Sölle at the Interface of Biblical Hermeneutic and Christian Spirituality* (Vienna: LIT Verlag, 2007).

10. See Mauritius Wilde, *Peter und Paulus: Wer in Gruppen entscheidet* [Peter and Paul: Who makes decisions in groups] (Münsterschwarzach: Vier Türme, 2003).

11. *St. Benedict's Rule*, 151.

12. *St. Benedict's Rule*, 46.

13. See "Dialogue Interreligieux Monastique—Monastic Interreligious Dialogue," accessible at www.dimmid.org (accessed October 10, 2018).

14. Pope John Paul II, *Redemptoris Missio: On the Permanent Validity of the Church's Missionary Mandate*, December 7, 1990. Available online at http://w2.vatican.va/content/john-paul-ii/en/encyclicals/documents/hf_jp-ii_enc_07121990_redemptoris-missio.html.

15. Abu Hamid Al-Ghazāli, *The Incoherence of the Philosophers*, trans. M.E. Marmura (Provo, UT: Brigham Young), 6 University, 2000.

16. Conrad Leyser and Hannah Williams, eds. *Mission and Monasticism* (Rome: Studia Anselmiana, 2013).

17. John W. Kiser, *The Monks of Tibhirine: Faith, Love, and Terror in Algeria* (New York: St. Martin's Griffin, 2003).

# CONCLUSION

1. See Mauritius Wilde, *Das neue Bild vom Gottesbild. Bild und Theologie bei Meister Eckhart* [The new image of God's image: Theology and image in the work of Meister Eckhart] (Freiburg, Switzerland: Freiburg University Press, 2000).

2. See chap. 8, where the term *mission* is discussed in greater detail.

3. Epistle of Mathetes to Diognetus, trans. Lightfoot and Harmer, 1981 translation, available online at http://www.earlychristianwritings .com/text/diognetus-lightfoot.html.